How Life Began

How Life Began

by

L. R. Croft

Lecturer in Biological Sciences
University of Salford

EVANGELICAL PRESS
12 Wooler Street, Darlington, Co. Durham, DL1 1RQ, England
© Evangelical Press
First published 1988

British Library Cataloguing in Publication Data

Croft, L.R. (Laurence Raymond)
    How life began.
    1. Life. Origins. Christian viewpoints
    I. Title
    261.5'5

ISBN 0-85234-254-3

Cover picture reproduced by courtesy of Cherry Valley Farms Limited

Typeset by JH Graphics Ltd, Reading
Printed by the Bath Press, Avon

Contents

Preface

Evolution is today taught as fact to our children from kindergarten onwards. By the time they reach adulthood they have become so indoctrinated that most give little thought to our Creator. Indeed many people today believe that God is superfluous to the modern world and that science has all the answers. I hope to show that this is not so. In this task I have limited my approach to a single problem, namely, the origin of life. This I believe holds the key, for without a naturalistic explanation of life's origin, the entire Darwinian edifice crumbles to a heap of nothingness.

There is no doubt that the materialistic view of the origin of life is deeply entrenched in modern thought. To take one popular school textbook, at random, we find it authoritatively stated that: 'Life arose on earth thousands of millions of years ago when collections of organic molecules in the primeval soup which formed in the primitive ocean became isolated from the bulk water of that ocean. Because of their closeness these molecules were able to interact with one another and began to show the first signs of life.'[1]

So widespread is this type of dogmatism that it is little wonder many of our young people have no belief in a Creator. Indeed I find that without exception the students with whom I come in contact are all convinced that life is the product of some great cosmic accident. For instance, one student, a freshman in the university, wrote of the origin of life: 'The theory which in my opinion is most likely is that of chemical evolution. It was suggested by a Russian scientist, Oparin, who said that the oceans and lakes were filled with a soup . . .' I must confess that I am astounded that Oparin (a dedicated Marxist) could have succeeded in converting most of Western society to his belief in the so-called 'primeval soup'. To illustrate how widespread is this belief, I will again quote from some of my students' essays. For instance: 'Oparin's theory does provide a well-explained account to the origin of life — the one which I personally support.' And another: 'Personally I tend to agree with the modern theory, because it seems so logical.' And a further one: 'I tend to go along with the theory suggested by Oparin. It is both logical and backed by experimental verification.'

It is principally for these young people that I have written this book. In it I hope to show that much of the so-called experimental evidence, on which their belief depends, has been deliberately exaggerated and distorted. Most students, indeed many scientists, are blissfully unaware of this fact. One of my students firmly believed that 'Once amino acids have formed there would be little difficulty in polymerizing them into proteins.' Another put it more bluntly: 'Billions of years went by and slowly these magic molecules evolved into all the organisms that fill the earth today.'

This is indeed blind faith — but in what? In the following pages I hope to show that the primeval soup theory has been the greatest scientific myth of all time. Furthermore, I hope to show that it has been mischievously perpetrated, for no other solid reason than to make us independent of a Creator. But my intention is not simply to demolish a scientific theory, for I have attempted to show that the latest scientific work, particularly that of molecular biology, provides convincing evidence for special creation.

L. R. Croft
Department of Biological Science
University of Salford
1988

Introduction

The central question concerning the origin of life is 'How did it arise from inanimate matter?' The conventional reply is that life appeared on the primeval earth by chance. Probably up to about a decade or so ago, most scientists would have gone along quite happily with this explanation. They would have argued, however, that although the chance formation of a living organism was unlikely, it was nevertheless within the realm of possibility. Today this is no longer the case. What has occurred during the last few years is a dramatic and somewhat unexpected transformation in our understanding of the living cell, the basic unit of all life. This has transpired because of the revolutionary new discoveries in molecular biology.

The situation today is such that a fair-minded scientist will concede that even the simplest living cell is so complex at a molecular level that it is not unlikely, but *impossible*, that an ancestral form could have arisen by chance alone. This situation could not have been foreseen. Indeed, one may recall a time in the late 1950s and early 1960s when it was widely held that the new science of molecular biology would pave the way for a complete understanding of how life arose from inanimate matter. It all seemed just a matter of time. Some scientists were so carried away by the general euphoria that they were foolish enough to talk openly of actually synthesizing life in a test tube. Ironically what has in fact happened is quite the reverse. Molecular biology of even the simplest cell has thrown back a curtain to reveal a much greater complexity and degree of organization than could have been anticipated two or three decades ago. The gulf that is now known

to exist between the living and non-living state is far greater
than anticipated and with each passing year it grows ever wider.
Consequently some scientists, including the molecular biologist
and Nobel prizewinner Francis Crick, have thrown up their
arms in despair and concluded that we shall never be able to
understand how life originated.

Other scientists seeking a naturalistic explanation for the
origin of life have resorted to theories that leave the realm of
science and verge on what should more properly be called science
fiction. Yet others, and to me these are more sinister, have
attempted to cloak the subject in a blanket of obscurantism.
The vast majority of scientists, however, prefer not to think
about the subject. Indeed, in my experience many are embar-
rassed even to talk about it. But it is far too important to ignore.
It is proper that it be brought out into the open. The entire
edifice of orthodox biology rests upon a mechanistic origin for
life. Indeed, the naturalistic explanation for the origin of life
is of absolute importance to Darwinism. Without chemical
evolution there can be no organic evolution and Darwin is dead
as the dodo.

In Darwin's day the cell was little understood. The techniques
for staining cell constituents had not been developed and the
cell was seen to be merely a blob of jelly, or 'protoplasm', to
use a term coined by T. H. Huxley.

So myopic was the view adopted by many scientists that they
sincerely believed they could create life in the laboratory. They
maintained that life could be generated from inanimate matter
on the injection of some 'vital spark'. Charles Darwin believed
(as did his grandfather before him) that this vital ingredient
was electricity. Indeed, Erasmus Darwin was the inspiration
for Mary Shelley's Frankenstein. All this is laughable in the
light of what we know today about the miraculous workings
of even the simplest cell.

The situation now is such that the basic philosophical questions regarding the nature of life, such as vitalism and spontaneous generation, which many believed had been laid to rest
a century or so ago, have now been revived and once again
have become topics for heated controversy. Spontaneous generation, however, is now dressed up in new apparel and is
presented under the guise of 'chemical evolution'. In essence

it is unchanged, being a reduction of all living creatures, all life, indeed everything, to a random coming together of inanimate matter. Chemical evolution, like biological evolution, is nothing other than gross materialism. This being so, it is not surprising to discover that its modern origins are in the writings of the Marxist biochemist Academician A. I. Oparin of the Soviet Union.

In 1924 Oparin published a small booklet entitled *The Origins of Life*, in which he extended Darwin's theory back from living organisms to supposedly the first chemicals on the primeval earth. Within the Soviet Union he was able to postulate what Darwin had shrunk from, namely, that not only had man evolved from lower forms of life, but that these themselves had arisen from inanimate matter. In essence life is merely an accident; God is finally dead and there is no meaning to existence.

Oparin's approach was both clever and devious. He was able to attract scientific attention for his hypothesis because he succeeded in turning a previously philosophical question into an experimental one. He showed that it was possible to do experiments in this field. Today his original experiments seem extremely naïve, but in the 1920s they were exactly what was being looked for. Several involved the study of droplets of organic material suspended in solution. He called these droplets 'coacervates', and he claimed they resembled the first protocells. He based this claim on the observation that the droplets could accumulate material added to the solution and that they would eventually split apart, or divide. This he claimed was analogous to the division of a living cell during mitosis. In fact it was nothing of the sort, for without the addition of substances from the outside the droplets would quickly cease to exist. Furthermore, as they lacked any informational content comparable with genetic material, their resemblance to living cells was minimal.

Oparin's coacervate concept has been widely circulated and is frequently found in a prominent position in many elementary textbooks. For some mysterious reason it has gained widespread acceptance. As I will argue in this book, it is but a will-o'-the-wisp, indeed a scientific hoax of the greatest magnitude.

The physicist Freeman Dyson has remarked: 'The Oparin

picture was generally accepted by biologists for half a century. It was popular not because there was any evidence to support it, but because it seemed to be the only alternative to Biblical creationism.'[1]

This view is echoed by Sir Fred Hoyle: 'It is remarkable that over the past half-century the scientific world has, almost without exception, believed a theory for which there is not a single supporting fact.'[2]

Throughout the Western world Oparin has achieved a remarkable following which at times has turned to reverence. He has done so by considerable cunning. Indeed, it is true to say that no other apostle of Marx has been so successful in the promulgation of his gospel of materialism. So it comes as no surprise to find that Oparin has been awarded the greatest honour of the Soviet Union. It is somewhat ironic to discover, however, that much of his success has been due to an Englishman, namely Professor J. B. S. Haldane.

Haldane, like Thomas Huxley and many other influential evolutionists, was a militant atheist. Haldane, however, preferred to pursue his goal under the cloak of socialism. The *Dictionary of National Biography* records: 'He was more interested in taking a swipe at God than at the ruling class.'[3]

Haldane entered the origin of life debate in 1929 when he published a short article in the *Rationalist Annual*, in which he introduced the notion that on the prebiotic earth large quantities of organic compounds would have formed and accumulated to give a 'hot dilute soup'. So began the myth of the primeval soup. Even more amazing is the fact that Haldane was not particularly serious when he made this simplistic suggestion. Indeed, he never expected it would ever be taken seriously.

Today the primeval soup idea, or a variant of it, is at the very heart of orthodox biology. It remains so because scientists, as Freeman Dyson has pointed out above, refuse to contemplate creation *ex nihilo*. Consequently for well over half a century the ridiculous primeval soup scenario has been branded as acceptable, despite the fact that it explains nothing and that there is no evidence to support it.

At the beginning of the nineteenth century the Rev. William Paley put forward his famous argument for the existence of a Creator based on evidence for design in nature. He used the now famous analogy of a man who, on finding a watch, could look at its intricate construction and deduce that it had been designed and built by a watchmaker. So too he argued with the natural world; we can, for example, see design in the construction of the vertebrate eye, and in the sting of the honey bee, to take just two of the many examples Paley used. Intelligent design is therefore proof of a Creator. Paley's argument was impeccable and for many years was the foundation stone of theistic science; that is, until Charles Darwin introduced the notion of natural selection, the blind watchmaker, as Richard Dawkins would prefer to call it. Thus organisms were no longer considered to have been constructed in a divine workshop but shaped according to the blind forces of nature.

Evidence for this scenario was provided by a particular interpretation of the fossil record. Although this was not in perfect agreement with what would have been predicted, it was nonetheless sufficient to convince most people that organisms had indeed gradually changed over a long period of time.

In this book I will revive Paley's argument and apply it to the molecular biology of the cell. Here we shall discover abundant evidence for intelligent design, but not for evolution. Unlike Paley's case, it cannot be refuted, as there is no demonstrable evidence that the cell has ever evolved. There are no intermediates between life and inanimate matter. We may conclude with Paley that 'What we are inspecting demonstrates, by its construction, contrivance and design. Contrivance must have had a contriver; design, a designer.'[4] Indeed, I hope to show that the whole of molecular biology speaks out loud and clear for intelligent design. Unfortunately, in the clamour of the modern world we have failed to recognize this.

1. The nature of life itself

The search for the origin of life has stimulated speculation and contention from the earliest of times. The early history of this debate centred around two distinct issues. The first was whether life could originate from inert matter — the so-called spontaneous generation controversy; and the second was whether life could be understandable solely in materialistic terms, a viewpoint adopted by those who opposed the doctrine of 'vitalism'. To appreciate how these ideas have developed we need to examine their backgrounds.

Spontaneous generation

The concept that life could spring from inert matter was a central part of Greek philosophy. Anaximander, the Greek Ionian philosopher, argued that living organisms developed from mud when it was exposed to the sun. For many centuries this belief was widely accepted. Aristotle, in particular, taught it and in so doing gave it respectability, so that it remained virtually unchallenged throughout ancient times, the Middle Ages and almost to the close of the seventeenth century. Lucretius wrote in the first century that 'The earth has gotten the name of mother, since all things are produced out of the earth. And many living creatures even now spring out of the earth.'

Towards the end of the seventeenth century scientists began to question this concept. Sir Robert Boyle, in particular, raised his voice against it in his *Sceptical Chymist* of 1661 and we find Leevwenhoek stating his disbelief in one of his letters of 1680.

The first main challenge to spontaneous generation came from experimental work carried out by the Italian Francesco Redi. His book *Experiments on the Generation of Insects*, published in 1688, was a best seller and went through five editions in twenty years. His challenge was successful because of the elegance and simplicity of his experiments. Up to Redi's time it was generally believed that complex organisms like worms and maggots arose from simpler materials such as mud and decaying meat. Thus we read in Shakespeare's *Antony and Cleopatra* (Act III, Sc.7):

> Your serpent of Egypt is bred now of your mud
> By the operation of your sun: so is your crocodile.

Redi observed that if meat was left exposed to the air for a few days it did indeed generate maggots, but if the meat was enclosed in a jar covered with fine cotton gauze no maggots developed. The meat, however, continued to putrefy — just as it did before. He correctly concluded that the maggots were not generated from the rotting meat but from eggs deposited on it by flies attracted by its odour. From this Redi developed his famous concept: '*Omne vivum ex vivo*', that is, 'No life without antecedent life.'

Redi's work, however, did not settle the issue and throughout the next century the spontaneous generation controversy remained an area of heated contention, until the turn of the century when the theory came under repeated attack from experimentalists who had adopted Redi's methodology. Important landmarks were Joblot's experiments and boiled hay infusions of 1718 and Carter's use of heat sterilization as a method for preserving food in around 1732.

At the turn of the eighteenth century the spontaneous generation of life debate began to adopt a slightly different format. Several people began to argue that maybe it was only the simplest forms of life that developed spontaneously, and that these subsequently developed into more sophisticated varieties. Leading this movement was Erasmus Darwin. In his long didactic poem *The Temple of Nature* published in 1803 he rambled on:

Organic Life beneath the shoreless waves
Was born, and nurs'd in Ocean's pearly caves;
First forms minute, unseen by spheric glass,
Move on the mud, or pierce the watery mass;
These, as successive generations bloom,
New powers acquire, and larger limbs assume . . .

Joseph Priestley immediately condemned such views, stating that 'If there be any such thing as atheism, this is certainly it.'[1] And so the debate continued throughout most of the nineteenth century until it was given the final *coup de grâce* by Louis Pasteur.

Pasteur entered the spontaneous generation debate shortly after the death of his much-loved daughter. Some have even suggested that he did so to exclude from his mind the painful memory of this tragedy. His experiments were of extreme simplicity. By using round-bottomed glass flasks constructed with a swan-shaped neck he found that heated broths would remain indefinitely without micro-organisms, whereas if the neck was snapped off, the clear nutrient broth soon became clouded, indicating the growth of organisms. These, argued Pasteur, had not been generated within the flask but had entered from the outside environment. These important experiments of Pasteur were published in 1862 and provided conclusive evidence that the fermentation of all infusions (i.e. nutrient broths) were mediated by living micro-organisms or 'germs' derived from the environment.

Pasteur was not only a great experimental scientist; he was also a versatile showman and a skilled propagandist. By using well-tried and proven tactics he was able to convince the Paris Académie des Sciences that micro-organisms abound in the atmosphere and do not arise *de novo* within the infusion.

One of Pasteur's formidable opponents was Pouchet, who failed to be convinced by these experiments. In a famous public debate Pouchet demonstrated that heating did not always prevent the appearance of microbes within the infusion. In this instance Pouchet had employed infusions of hay and it was left to the English scientist John Tyndall to demonstrate that hay infusions always contained spores which were not killed even after prolonged heating.

At the time of Pasteur's birth in 1822 the average life-span in European countries was around forty years. In some communities it was as low as twenty-five, yet by the time of Pasteur's death in 1895 life expectancy for many had reached the biblical three score years and ten. To attribute this entirely to Pasteur is probably an exaggeration, but it is undoubtedly true that a considerable part of it was due to his application of the scientific method to medicine.

It is ironic that in the very year Pasteur entered the spontaneous generation debate, in England Charles Darwin published his *Origin of Species*, which required life to have originated by some form of spontaneous generation. That Darwinism developed with the significant implication that life originated from inert matter at the very time when many felt that the doctrine of spontaneous generation had been buried once and for all introduced considerable confusion into the debate and this has persisted ever since.

The popular view that Pasteur's work destroyed the spontaneous generation theory has only recently been contested by John Farley in his book *The Spontaneous Generation Controversy* (1977). Farley argues that the debate did not cease following Pasteur's work but that during the last decades of the nineteenth century it died a natural death. This he believes was due to the immense expansion of activity within all the sciences that occurred at that time. Scientists, in other words, had plenty of other things to do than engage in a debate that many of them had grown tired of.

Vitalism

Vitalism is the philosophical belief that living matter cannot be understood solely in terms of the laws of chemistry and physics. For many centuries vitalists argued that chemicals obtained from living organisms were fundamentally different from those obtained from minerals. Somewhere in their structure they held a mysterious life-force, the *élan vital*. This belief was so powerful that the early physical scientists divided chemical substances into two groups. The first were those obtained from natural materials that at some time in their history had 'lived'.

These were called 'organic'. The second group were those substances prepared from minerals and which had never previously been part of a life-cycle. These were termed 'inorganic'.

Berzelius, the most famous of the early chemists, was a vitalist and believed that all organic substances were produced under the influence of a 'vital force'. This being so, he argued that it was not possible to make them artificially within the laboratory.

Most textbooks contain the misleading story of Wöhler destroying the vital force theory by synthesizing urea, one of the most ubiquitous biological substances, from inorganic chemicals. This is one of those myths that haunt the history of science. What Wöhler accomplished in 1828 was to synthesize urea by heating cyanic acid with ammonia to give ammonium cyanate, which on further heating turned into urea.

$$NH_4\ NCO \xrightarrow{\text{heat}} NH_2\ CO\ NH_2$$

ammonium cynate

urea

Wöhler did not claim to have destroyed the doctrine of vitalism, for he knew that his starting materials had in fact been prepared, not from inorganic sources, but from biological material. Cyanic acid had been prepared by heating dried blood with potash and iron. Thus, contrary to popular belief, Wöhler did not destroy vitalism. The early concept died a natural death, neither sudden nor dramatic, by the steady accumulation of contradictory fact.

However, a residual belief in vitalism has lingered on even until recent times. If we look at the history of organic chemistry over the last 150 years one discovers that there have been many occasions when the question whether or not the properties of a substance may be totally explicable in purely naturalistic terms has been brought to the fore. In 1926 J. B. Sumner claimed he had obtained the enzyme urease in crystalline form. Immediately he met intense and bitter opposition. Enzymes were seen to be an integral component of life and it seemed unacceptable to many that they should have properties similar to other organic substances. Sumner's claims were doubted for many years and it was not until 1946, twenty years after his discovery, that the truth was finally recognized and he was awarded the Nobel Prize for his achievement.

The ultimate ambition of the materialist is to synthesize life in the laboratory. Only when this is accomplished will he feel that vitalism is finally defeated. Chemists have therefore gone on to synthesize larger and larger natural molecules. In 1965 tremendous excitement was created when a group of Chinese scientists achieved the first chemical synthesis of the protein insulin. To many this was viewed as the first step on the road towards the chemical synthesis of life. Although one cannot fail to be impressed by the achievements of organic chemistry, to extrapolate them to this ultimate goal is foolishness of the greatest magnitude. J. B. S. Haldane speculated in 1965 that 'Some of us, or the next generation, will try to make a living organism . . . I think it will happen in some of your lifetimes.'[2] These are the words of a hardened materialist who has been carried away by his ideology into cloud-cuckoo land.

Darwin and the origin of life

During the second half of the last century Darwinism drove at the very heart of the vitalism-spontaneous generation debate. Darwinists argued that the evolution of species had occurred by random natural selection following the *chance* formation of the first life form. Incredibly this was a return to the spontaneous generation theory that many scientists had fought hard and long to silence. Darwin was well aware that a satisfactory explanation for the origin of life was of crucial importance to his theory. Undoubtedly he recognized that this was the weakest link in his theory. On the other hand, his early opponents, rather than accept defeat, found that here was a position whereby they might compromise with evolution. They argued that if God created the first living cell to contain the instructions for evolution, then the Christian need not surrender his faith. The Genesis account of creation could be believed by interpreting the days to be aeons of time. Darwin in fact had himself realized that this might be a subtle way of getting acceptance for his theory. Thus we find in the early editions of the *Origin of Species* the concluding paragraph: 'There is grandeur in this view of life, with its several powers, having been originally breathed by the Creator into a few forms or into one . . .'[3]

Darwin's dishonesty is apparent. He had long been an atheist and had inserted the above paragraph to lessen the tumult he knew his book would create. He no more believed in a Creator than he did in a flat earth.

In retrospect one can see that the question of the origin of life was the Achilles heel of Darwinism that his critics failed to exploit. When the German zoologist H. G. Brown wrote to Darwin on this issue, he received the following reply: 'I cannot see the force of your objection that nothing is effected until the origin of life is explained.'[4] Darwin concluded his letter by saying that he thought it likely that life could be created from inanimate matter by the application of electricity. This was by no means a new suggestion. Experimenters had long claimed that living creatures might be made in the laboratory by electricity. In 1837 Andrew Crosse believed he had created an eight-legged monster which he named *Arcarus Electricus* by passing an electric current through a mixture of potassium silicate and hydrochloric acid. And, as we have mentioned previously, Erasmus Darwin had claimed similar feats of creation.

Charles Darwin has been claimed by many of his followers to have been the greatest English scientist since Newton. For him to resurrect his grandfather's idea, (indeed the same procedure employed by Shelley's Frankenstein), that inanimate matter could be sparked into life by electricity, either indicates his stupidity, or shows the desperate plight of his theory over this crucial issue.

It is clear that Darwin and his contemporaries viewed living cells as mere blobs of jelly. They had no knowledge of subcellular structure or organization. To them any blob of inert matter might be jerked into life by a spark of electricity. Probably many of them had watched a frog's leg jump when connected to a source of electricity. To many of these scientists, including Darwin, the vital force of life was nothing other than electricity.

One of the earliest Darwinists to research the origin of life was H. Charlton Bastian, Professor of Medicine at University

College, London. In his book *The Origin of Life* (1911) he reviewed the situation thus: 'Concerning the main question — that of the Origin of Life on this Earth — men of science, or at least a majority of them, no longer appeal to the intervention of any non-natural or miraculous cause. As believers in the Doctrine of Evolution they are content to suppose that at some time after the fiery heat of the crust of our globe had sufficiently cooled to permit of the deposition of water upon its surface, there must have been a further continuance of the physico-chemical processes . . . their result was the production of what we now know as "living matter".'[5]

Bastian was convinced of the continuous and spontaneous generation of life. Over a long period he conducted a large number of experiments which he believed demonstrated the continuous creation of life. Bastian was no charlatan for he had the highest scientific credentials. In essence what he did was to take various salt solutions, seal them in glass tubes and heat them at 130°C. After cooling they were allowed to remain at room temperature for several weeks. Following this they were opened and examined for micro-organisms. His findings were published in a series of books which display innumerable microphotographs of the microbes he discovered. It is apparent to us today that although he had taken strenuous steps to exclude the possibility of contamination, he had clearly failed!

Bastian was a victim of his age. If there had been better techniques for detecting micro-organisms he would never have made his enormous blunder. There is no excuse today for similar fiascos, yet incredibly there are many scientists who still believe in the continuous and spontaneous creation of life. They maintain that in certain unique sites on the earth inanimate matter assembles together spontaneously to form life. One suggested site is the thermal springs of the Kuril Islands. Another suggestion favours the deep hydrothermal vents of the mid-ocean ridges. The Atlantis II deep brine ridge is thought to be an especially promising location. Here some scientists believe life is continuously formed today.[6]

Dr C. Ponnamperuma, Director of the Laboratory of Chemical Evolution of the University of Maryland, has concluded in an article written for the *New Scientist* magazine of May 1982 that 'There is mounting evidence from our current experience of the hydrothermal vents of the ocean floor, near the Galapagos Islands, that life may be arising from inanimate matter — abiogenesis — at this very moment.' [7]

So we find that as we edge towards the end of the twentieth century, scientists still linger after a belief in spontaneous generation. This latest episode is a particularly pointless adventure, for if micro-organisms are discovered — so what? Micro-organisms exist over the entire planet, indeed they occur in the most unlikely places, but they do not arrive there by a process of spontaneous generation. As Thomas Hardy once wrote, 'That which are called advanced ideas are really in great part but the latest fashion . . .' [8]

The fundamental problem — the origin of life — is the cornerstone of all evolutionary enquiry. Yet surprisingly it is rarely given the attention it merits. Even long after Darwinism became the lintel of orthodox biological theory, the nature of the origin of life remained neglected. As we have discussed above, Darwin himself was dismissive on the issue and was even prepared to be dishonest.

If continuous and spontaneous creation are dismissed, the evolutionist has no other alternative than to maintain that life arose, not continuously, but at one definite point in the history of the earth. This is what the vast majority of scientists accept today. Yet there are innumerable and formidable problems associated with the acceptance of this view. These will be reviewed in subsequent chapters. At this point let us enumerate them.

1. What was the nature of the earth's early atmosphere? An atmosphere like the present one is oxidizing and could not have led to life.

2. If biomolecules were generated spontaneously on the primeval earth, how did they arise? And, more importantly, how did they reach sufficient concentration and purity for life to develop?

3. Enzymes are essential for all life. Life is not possible without enzymes, so how could life have arisen without enzymes? This is a classic chicken and egg situation, to which the evolutionist has no answer.

4. Most biomolecules are chiral, (i.e. 'left-or right-handed') and chirality is intricately associated with life. But how did chiral discrimination originate in cells?

5. How did the first cell arise? How did it learn to divide and multiply? How did the complex mechanism of cell reproduction arise? Logically it must have occurred in the brief period of the first cell's existence and viability — but this is impossible.

6. How did the simple prokaryotes develop into the more complex eukaryotic organisms?

All of these problems pose formidable difficulties for the evolutionist; so much so, that the origin of life problem is largely hidden beneath a bushel. It is rarely discussed or debated. Many fear that if it were brought out into the open then the proverbial cat would be let out of the bag.

It is indeed extremely perplexing to realize that although Darwinism is the central doctrine of orthodox biology, the key problem of the origin of life remains unsolved. It is not satisfactory to shrink away from it and maintain that it is too difficult a problem to solve. It is so fundamental to the evolutionary scenario that one cannot see how it is possible to proceed without a reasonable explanation being found. Yet the fact remains that the scientific community continues to work and preach the gospel of Darwin regardless.

2. The chemistry of life

The argument presented in this book does require a basic understanding of the chemistry of living organisms. We normally call this area of science 'biochemistry'. Biochemistry is a relatively new science which during the past two decades has undergone enormous expansion. It is an extremely complex subject but I believe that this need not intimidate the reader who is unfamiliar with the particular jargon involved. For many years I have taught this subject to students of widely differing backgrounds and I have discovered that although the subject may seem daunting, in fact, it may be boiled down to a basic core from which it is possible to grasp most of the essential concepts. (Please refer to the Appendix.)

Proteins

The proteins are the most diverse and abundant of all biological molecules. In each cell there are at least 2000 different proteins. These vary in molecular weight from several thousand to many million. They also have an enormous range of functions. Some are enzymes and are essential for cell metabolism; others have a passive structural role. All proteins contain the elements carbon, hydrogen, nitrogen and oxygen. Most, but not all, also contain sulphur; a small number contain phosphorus and a handful contain inorganic elements such as iron, zinc and copper.

All proteins consist of long chains of amino acids linked together by so-called 'peptide bonds'. Peptide bonds are formed

when the amino group (NH_2) of one amino acid is condensed
with the acid, i.e. carboxyl group, of a second amino acid,
with the loss of a molecule of water, thus:

The peptide bond thus formed has the structure:

In the above example the product was the *dipeptide*, alanylglycine. If the process of joining amino acids on were to be continued the next peptide would be a *tripeptide*, then a *tetrapeptide* and so on. Most proteins have at least 200 amino acids joined together by peptide bonds to give a single chain. Probably the most amazing discovery made in science this century was the finding that proteins are built up of amino acids put together in a specific and unique order. This was a most profound and largely unexpected discovery. To appreciate its significance let us look at a couple of examples. Let us start with the dipeptide formed between alanine and glycine. There are two possibilities, either alanine-glycine or glycine-alanine. For a tripeptide formed from the amino acids glycine, alanine and leucine, there are a total of six possible combinations:

> glycine - alanine - leucine
> glycine - leucine - alanine
> leucine - glycine - alanine
> leucine - alanine - glycine
> alanine - glycine - leucine
> alanine - leucine - glycine

If we now look at a relatively simple protein with about 200 amino acids then the number of possible permutations is enormous. In fact, calculations have indicated that if only one molecule of each possible sequence existed then the weight of the total would far exceed the weight of the entire earth!

The discovery in 1955 that each protein contained amino acids held together in a specific and unique order was of major importance. It was this finding that gave impetus to the elucidation of the molecular biology of heredity. Further work in the 1960s and 1970s involving studies on protein crystals revealed that not only did proteins have a unique order of amino acids but that the peptide chain formed folded up in a unique way to give a three-dimensional structure. The folding of linear chains of amino acids into highly organized structures is the key to understanding the multitude of functions these molecules are able to undertake.

The functional variety of proteins is immense. Haemoglobin is the oxygen-carrying protein of blood; hair fibres and finger nails are made of the protein keratin; insulin is a protein hor-

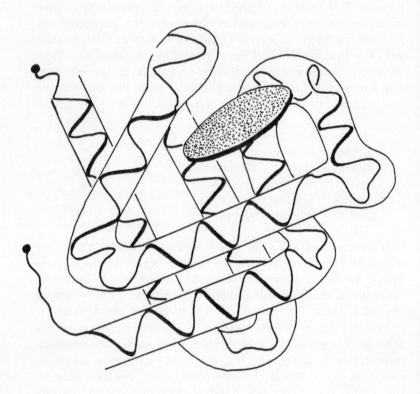

FIGURE 1

Structural features of a haemoglobin subunit showing
the folding of the polypeptide chain and the position of
the haem group. Haemoglobin itself consists of four of
these units.

mone, deficiency of which results in diabetes; milk contains the protein casein; Factor VIII is a protein needed for blood clotting; skin contains the protein collagen; gamma-globulin is an antibody protein present in serum; digestive juices contain protein enzymes; the protein melittin is responsible for the pain following a bee sting; and you are reading this book due to the fact that light can pass through the collagen of your cornea, then through the crystallin proteins of the lens eventually reaching the protein rhodopsin of the retina, from which a signal is transmitted to the proteins of the brain. Proteins are therefore ubiquitous and life is inconceivable without them.

Enzymes

An intriguing feature of the many and varied chemical reactions that occur within living cells is that they take place very much more rapidly than similar reactions carried out in a test tube. Let us take, as an example, the digestion of meat protein. Suppose one evening we have grilled steak for dinner: by the time we are ready to retire, most of the meat will have been broken down into its constituent amino acids, which will have begun to be distributed throughout the tissues of the body. All this will have been accomplished at a body temperature of 37°C, yet to do the same thing in the laboratory would require heating the meat with concentrated acid, at about 110°C, for at least twenty-four hours. Our bodies are able to accomplish the feat more easily because enzymes are present in digestive juices.

Enzymes are therefore biological catalysts that are able to increase the rates of specific chemical reactions and remain unchanged afterwards. They are amongst the most important molecules of life.

Today most people are aware of enzymes since their appearance in washing powders. However, they have been used by man since the earliest of times, for example, in alcohol production and in cheese manufacture. Indeed one of man's earliest technological steps was the discovery that yeast cells are capable of converting sugars into alcohol. Probably the process was discovered accidentally; today it may be seen to represent man's first venture into what we now call 'biotechnology'.

The first scientific study of enzymes goes back to Louis Pasteur, who investigated the mechanism of fermentation. Enzymes at that time were known as 'ferments' and they were believed to be associated intimately with living cells. It was in 1897 that Edward Buchner demonstrated that sugars could be fermented with a cell-free extract of yeast. This discovery paved the way for the detailed study of enzymes as biomolecules. Yet it was not until 1926 that the first enzyme was obtained sufficiently pure for it to be crystallized. This was accomplished by James Sumner working with the enzyme urease. This particular discovery met with considerable controversy. It was only after many more enzymes were obtained in crystalline form that the majority of scientists accepted that enzymes were indeed only complex protein molecules. Now many hundreds of enzymes have been isolated and studied. In particular the last few decades have witnessed tremendous advances in our knowledge of them. Yet the simple finding that all enzymes are proteins took much painstaking research to establish.

Many enzymes have a name terminating with the suffix 'ase', thus we have 'pronase', an enzyme that breaks down protein; 'urease' the enzyme that hydrolyses urea; 'cellulase' the enzyme that breaks down cellulose, and so on. One can also see from this that the first part of the name for the enzyme is derived from the substance on which it acts, thus pronase attacks protein, urease urea and cellulase cellulose. Occasionally an enzyme will only function if there is another type of molecule present. This molecule is called a 'co-enzyme'. Co-enzymes are usually small molecules and are from a wide variety of substances.

Enzymes are incredibly efficient catalysts, far more efficient than anything that could be invented in the laboratory. One of the most spectacular enzymes is catalase, which is present in all living cells, where its function is to destroy hydrogen peroxide. A dilute solution of hydrogen peroxide if left around at room temperature will slowly break down into water and oxygen thus:

$$2 \ H_2O_2 \longrightarrow 2 \ H_2O + O_2$$

Celery is a particularly rich source of catalase. If a small piece of celery is chopped up and the juice squeezed from it, then added to a solution of hydrogen peroxide, the latter decomposes with almost explosive violence. This happens so spectacularly because of the enzyme catalase which is able to break down the hydrogen peroxide many millions of times faster than the uncatalysed reaction.

The presence of catalase in all cells, even dead cells, poses particular problems to the detergent industry. Hydrogen peroxide is included in detergents in order to bleach clothes during washing and so produce that brighter-than-white impression. Catalase is inevitably present on soiled clothes from dead skin cells and so on. Yet the minute amount present is sufficient to destroy all the peroxide present in the detergent. Detergent manufacturers would dearly wish that enzymes were not as efficient as they are!

Another example of the remarkable efficiency of enzymes is in the nitrogen fixation of plants. Due to the presence of specific enzymes, nitrogen can be converted into plant tissue by reactions occurring at normal temperatures and atmospheric pressure. To accomplish the same in the chemical industry needs special metal-catalysts and operational temperatures of around 500°C with pressures of about 400 atmospheres. If ICI could develop a process for nitrogen fixation comparable to that of the natural enzymic process, their shares would rocket sky-high on the Stock Exchange.

Enzymes are not only highly efficient catalysts, they are also very specific in their action. Thus if the enzyme arginase (which breaks down the amino acid arginine) is added to a solution containing arginine together with 101 other amino acids, it will specifically go for only the arginine molecules and ignore all the others. This remarkable specificity is best illustrated with the enzyme urease. Urease reacts specifically with urea thus:

$$NH_2 \; CO \; NH_2 \quad \longrightarrow \quad NH_3 + CO_2$$
$$\text{urease}$$

Now if instead of urea, methyl urea $CH_3 \; NH \; CO \; NH_2$ is used, then there is no reaction. This indicates that the enzyme urease is specific only for urea and absolutely nothing else.

We normally refer to the substance acted on by the enzyme as the 'substrate'. From a molecular point of view we say that *only* the substrate can fit exactly into the reaction region of the enzyme molecule. This region is known as the 'active site'. We could think of this in terms of a lock and key analogy but a better one is to think of the enzyme as a jig-saw puzzle where only one piece is needed to complete the picture. When taken the last piece (i.e. substrate) will be found to fit precisely into the vacant position. Let us take this analogy further. Suppose someone were unlucky enough to have purchased a jig-saw puzzle that had one piece missing (a particularly galling situation for the dedicated jig-saw puzzle fanatic). Suppose he were to rush out and purchase another identical puzzle. Let us say it had 1000 pieces; then he would be forced to go through each of these in turn until he found the missing piece. Maybe in the process he might try to force another piece into the vacancy. It might be possible but the resulting picture would be terribly wrong. So with an enzyme, there could be a thousand different molecules in a cell but only one will exactly fit into the active site. What is amazing is that the enzyme, unlike the jig-saw fanatic, is able to locate the particular molecule instantly. How it does this is still a mystery.

Many elementary biology textbooks now display so-called metabolic pathways showing the many enzymes involved in the workings of a living cell. At least 2000 different enzymes are involved. These charts are extremely complex and to many they simply boggle the mind. The resulting complex interplay of all these biomolecules is life. Enzymes are therefore an essential feature of all life and life is impossible without them. Even the simplest form of life, as we know it today, has an extremely complex and interlocking metabolism that involves several thousand enzymes. The question we are now concerned with in this book is how could even the simplest metabolism have formed from inanimate matter? The simple fact that there are no extant intermediates between the non-living and living state is strong evidence that life has not evolved as is generally supposed. (Viruses were at one time thought to be intermediary between life and inanimate matter. But this is no longer thought to be so.) Indeed the very fact that life is known to be a complex interplay, involving thousands of different enzymes giving it a metabolism, speaks out loud and clear against a gradual evolution.

Nucleic acids

There are two sorts of nucleic acid. One is *Ri*bo*n*ucleic *A*cid (RNA) and the other is *D*eoxyribo*n*ucleic *A*cid (DNA). Their names come from the fact that they are found within the nucleus of cells of higher organisms. The 'acid' part of their names arises from the fact that they contain phosphoric acid. Both types of nucleic acid are long chains of sugar molecules linked together by phosphoric acid which acts like a connecting bridge. DNA and RNA differ in that the sugar in RNA is ribose whereas in DNA it is 2-deoxyribose. On each sugar is found an organic base; in RNA this is either guanine, adenine, uracil or cytosine (abbreviated G, A, U, C), whereas in DNA the bases are the same except that uracil is replaced by thymine (T). The basic structural units are therefore:

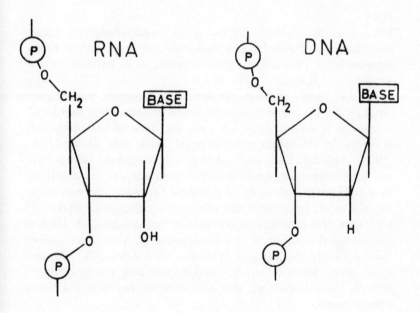

Nucleic acids are therefore polymers built on the general principle:

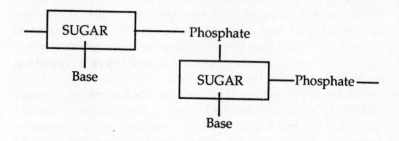

The linkage between sugar molecules is exactly the same in both RNA and DNA, being between the 3' and 5' positions. Although other linkages are possible these do not occur.

DNA
DNA has a uniform backbone of sugar-phosphate-sugar-phosphate . . . etc. In any molecule this may repeat many thousands of time. The genetic message is carried by the sequence of bases.

In 1953 James Watson, an American biologist, and Francis Crick, a British research student, together discovered that DNA existed as a double helix. A racy acccount of this discovery is given in Watson's controversial book *The Double Helix* (1968). Although they were subsequently awarded a Nobel Prize much bitterness surrounds this episode in science. For one thing they 'borrowed' the results of Rosalind Franklin who was working in another university (and who later died tragically of cancer) and those of the American biochemist Erwin Chargaff. He had discovered that in any DNA the amount of A always equalled· that of T, and the amount of G that of C. Chargaff, who had spent many years in tedious and painstaking research before deducing this simple fact, was later to write bitterly of the Nobel prizewinners.

Thus DNA consists of two chains twisted about each other forming a double helix. The chains are linked together by weak hydrogen bonding between the pairs of bases A ⟶ T and G ➔ C. Although these individual bonds are relatively weak, when there are several thousand of them in a long DNA molecule they give a cumulative bonding of considerable strength. Thus the DNA molecule is relatively stable which, of course, is essential for a substance needed to carry the genetic message. Of course, DNA is a very long molecule but within the cell's nucleus it is very much folded up into a compact structure. A good analogy is a length of wool being wrapped up to form a compact ball.

The fact that DNA consists of a double helical structure means that the genetic message is essentially recorded twice. Thus in one chain if there is an A then the complementary chain must carry a T, and where there is a G the corresponding chain would have a C and so on. One consequence of this is that the chains of DNA must be anti-parallel. The directions of the sugar-phosphate backbones must run in opposite directions. Thus a simplified view of the double helix of DNA showing the anti-parallel direction of the chains and the base-pairing rules is as shown in Figure 2.

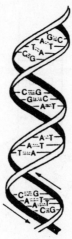

FIGURE 2

The Double Helix of DNA. This consists of two nucleotide chains running in opposite directions and held together by hydrogen bonding. In eukaryotic cells the DNA is complexed with protein.

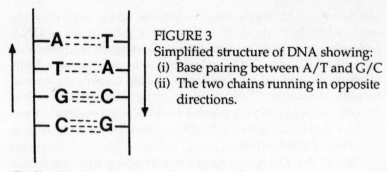

FIGURE 3
Simplified structure of DNA showing:
 (i) Base pairing between A/T and G/C
 (ii) The two chains running in opposite
      directions.

Replication

One reason for the immediate acceptance of the structure of
DNA was that it provided a simple explanation for the transmission of genetic information such as occurs during cell replication. In this the double-helical structure of DNA is superb
for its simplicity. Thus because of the base-pairing rules if the
double helix was prized open the two separate chains could
now readily be copied providing the necessary nucleotide
components and enzymes were available.

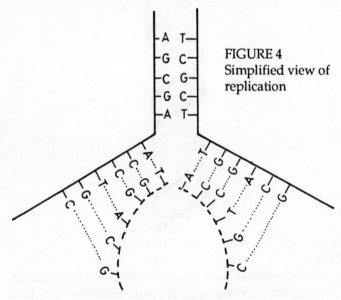

FIGURE 4
Simplified view of
replication

Formation of new chains

So we now see that each daughter double helix consists of half the old helix and half an entirely new one. The daughter helices are now identical to the original parent; they have therefore been replicated.

The whole process is both elegant and simple. But one should bear in mind that this is only a bare outline and only a very superficial description. In actual fact replication in the cells of higher organisms is barely understood. It is certainly a very complex process that involves a large number of specific enzymes. For one thing it is necessary to unwind the double helix before replication can occur. This is an extremely complex process of which we know only the barest details. Further enzymes are needed to snip open the helix at certain positions.

A small length of RNA is needed to initiate the entire process which subsequently must be removed and replaced by an equivalent piece of DNA. The DNA chain is made initially in only small fragments and subsequently connected together. All these steps require separate enzymes which must be available and regulated to ensure that the process of replication goes on smoothly. Furthermore as the two chains of DNA run in opposite directions then the synthesis must proceed simultaneously in opposite senses.

The simple idea of replication put forward by Watson and Crick in the 1950s is now known to be very much an oversimplification. Replication of even the smallest fragment of DNA requires more than twenty specific proteins and enzymes, each one necessary for an integral part of the whole process.

RNA

RNA differs from DNA in having one extra oxygen atom in its sugar molecule. This simple difference has tremendous significance in its properties. In particular it is very much more unstable than DNA. There are several different forms of RNA within the cell: ribosomal RNA (rRNA) 80%, which go to make up the structure of the ribosomes of the cell, i.e. the site for protein synthesis; transfer RNA (tRNA) 15%; and messenger RNA (mRNA) 5%.

Transfer RNA (tRNA) is a relatively small single-stranded nucleic acid that folds up into an intricate but stable structure. Part of it, which is exposed, is known as the 'anti-codon' and

its function is to match up with the '*codon*' on a messenger RNA.
Each codon consists of three adjacent bases which together code
for a particular amino acid. In all there are sixty-four different
codons that are able to code for a total of twenty amino acids.
It is useful to use the analogy of language and think of nucleic
acids as a language using bases, divided up into groups of
codons, and proteins as another language made up of amino
acids. Translation may occur from one to the other and the
'dictionary' linking nucleic acid language to that of proteins we
refer to as the 'genetic code' (this will be discussed in detail
in a subsequent chapter).

Messenger RNA (mRNA) carries the genetic message from
the DNA in the cell nucleus to the cytoplasm, where it links
up to the ribosome and is subsequently 'translated' into protein. It is a linear molecule and is relatively unstable, which
is important as this fact is part of the regulation mechanism
for protein synthesis within the cell.

The third form of RNA within the cell is ribosomal RNA
(rRNA). This occurs in the ribosomes which are the protein-
synthesizing factories of the cell. These are essentially complex
structures consisting of two components, a large subunit and
a small subunit. Both subunits contain ribosomal RNA
molecules of high molecular weight together with a large number
of unique protein molecules.

3. Myth of the primeval soup

Introduction

The first experiments designed to discover whether biomolecules could have formed spontaneously on the primeval earth were carried out towards the close of the nineteenth century. It was discovered that electric discharges in the presence of carbon dioxide and water gave rise to formaldehyde. At this time it was widely held that formaldehyde was the initial product of photosynthesis and so it was considered reasonable that if this substance had formed on the primitive earth, it should have been spontaneously converted into sugar molecules. At the time this was seen by many to be a vital clue to the formation of life on earth.

Biologists like Sir Ray Lankester took this a step further and proposed that sheets of a protoplasm-like material would have formed over pools of water and life eventually would have developed. Baly of Liverpool University demonstrated that in the absence of chlorophyll (essential for photosynthesis) chemicals like ammonia, methane and water could combine together in sunlight to form simple substances such as sugar molecules. However, it was not until after the Second World War that interest in this subject was revived.

In 1950 Professor Melvin Calvin, of the University of California, demonstrated that formic acid and formaldehyde were produced when solutions of carbon dioxide and water were irradiated with α-particles. This was found to take place in the absence of chlorophyll. Interest intensified and in 1952 Harold Urey, of the University of Chicago, suggested to one of his research students that he might like to mimic the primordial atmosphere and examine if an input of energy would produce biological-type molecules. Urey argued that the primitive atmosphere must have been anaerobic (that is without oxygen) and was therefore reducing. The research student was Stanley Miller and the experiment he devised has become a landmark in the history of the study of the origin of life. [1]

Miller's experiments

Miller's 1953 experiment was extremely simple, both in concept and operation. The apparatus (see illustration opposite) consisted of two pyrex glass flasks connected in a closed circuit. In one of the flasks were inserted a pair of tungsten electrodes across which could be discharged sparks of about 60,000 volts. In the second flask water, which had been carefully sterilized, to ensure no micro-organisms were present, was continually boiled. Into this apparatus were pumped the gases methane, hydrogen and ammonia — a plausible primeval atmosphere.

The set-up was maintained for about a week, after which the products formed were examined. The most obvious product was large quantities of a yellow polymer which turned out to be colloidal silica, produced by the action of the ammonia on the silica glass apparatus. Apart from this there were small quantities of simple organic substances, including succinic acid, lactic acid, formic acid, acetic acid, propionic acid, glycollic acid, urea, methylurea and a number of simple amino acids. The main amino acids were glycine and alanine, with lesser amounts of aspartic acid, glutamic acid, β-alanine and sarcosine. That these had not been formed by contamination with micro-organisms was demonstrated by repeating the experiment with the same gases but without sparking. Under these circumstances no amino acids formed.

The mechanism whereby amino acids are formed in Miller's apparatus is believed to be via the first formation of an aldehyde, followed by reaction of this with ammonia, to give an amino acid. In organic chemistry this is known as the Strecker synthesis. As all who have carried out a Strecker synthesis in the laboratory will confirm, if the components are not carefully measured out

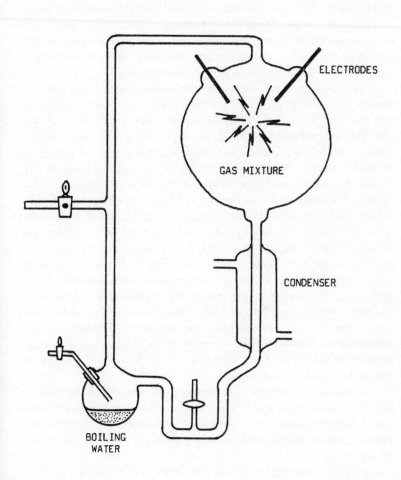

FIGURE 5

Apparatus used by Stanley Miller in his famous primeval soup experiment. Gases circulated through the apparatus during which sparks were passed across the tungsten electrodes in the large flask. The products were condensed and collected in the smaller flask.

correctly and heated at a precise temperature, the product is a tarry 'goo'. Such a 'goo' was obtained in Miller's experiment.

The publication of Miller's finding caused unprecedented excitement. Soon many other scientists were performing similar experiments and a small cottage industry of primeval-soup workers was busily creating new concoctions.

Many investigators were able to demonstrate that similar results occurred even when another source of energy replaced the electric discharge. Thus when gas mixtures were passed through a furnace at 1000°C, or exposed to ultraviolet light, similar tars and goos were produced. Furthermore, the presence of amino acids could be demonstrated in them. However, it should be pointed out that amino acids were particularly easy to detect because of the availability of highly sensitive automatic amino acid analysers. The main amino acids detected invariably were glycine (NH_2 CH_2 COOH) together with traces of alanine (NH_2 $CH(CH_3)COOH$). Any other amino acid was present in an extremely minute amount. It must be pointed out, however, that all these amino acids were racemic mixtures (i.e. containing a mixture of the 'right-handed' and 'left-handed' versions) and so do not resemble those found in proteins. And, more importantly, the majority of them do not belong to the family of twenty amino acids that occur in natural protein molecules. The significance of Miller's findings is therefore highly questionable.

Nevertheless, the type of experiment demonstrated by Miller has been used as a model by many subsequent investigators and a large industry has developed with chemists maltreating various gas mixtures and having a field day in analysing the products.

One major landmark in all this work has been the finding that not only are amino acids formed, but also the bases needed to construct nucleic acids. In 1960 J. Oró demonstrated that the base adenine is produced, albeit in poor yield, when an aqueous solution of ammonium cyanate is heated at 90°C for several days. Although there is little doubt that with the reducing atmosphere scenario ammonium cyanate would indeed have been present on the primeval earth, it is more difficult to conceive how a solution of it would have become concentrated enough for adenine to form. Leslie Orgel has argued that instead of concentration by evaporation, slow freezing of the primeval soup would have led to the concentration of products in the lower layers.

Other nucleic acid bases have also been discovered in this type of experiment, but again only at extremely low concentration. The pyrimidine bases, cytosine, uracil and thymine, have all been found at low concentration. The most unlikely base to be formed under these circumstances is the purine base guanine. Yet this molecule is essential for the construction of nucleic acid.

Specific criticism

It is extremely doubtful whether the products formed in the primeval ocean would have reached sufficient concentration for chemical reactions to have occurred. Thermodynamic calculations indicate that organic compounds formed in the atmosphere would have been largely destroyed by ultraviolet light and so would never have reached the oceans. [2] Accordingly, the concentration of amino acids, for instance, in the primordial soup would have been about the same as in the oceans today. Consequently many chemists have become pessimistic and have talked openly about the 'myth' of the primeval soup.

Even if one were to shift everything from the oceans to the land surface, this is still unhelpful. Ultraviolet light would have made the rock surfaces highly oxidizing, (as occurs on the surface of Mars), so that any organic substance coming into contact with them would quickly be destroyed. Organic biomolecules would therefore have had an ephemeral existence on land.

This leads to a major problem. Even if substances were formed on the primeval earth, how could they have been purified sufficiently to take part in organic synthesis? Dr G. Cairns-Smith has commented: 'No sensible organic chemist would hope to get much out of a reaction from starting materials that were tars containing the reactants as minor constituents.' [3]

As all chemistry students know, practical organic chemistry is neither easy nor possible without pure starting materials. To suggest that complicated organic molecules could be produced from the *minor* constituents of tars and 'goos' is one of the most foolish and idiotic notions of twentieth-century science!

Furthermore, one always has the nagging doubt that the much-quoted primeval soup experiments are not wholly representative of the many experiments that must have been performed over the years. It is almost certain that only those experiments producing the desired result have in fact been published. The upshot is that the significance of many of the experiments is less than one would suppose. The fact that simple biomolecules have been obtained by careful analysis of soup 'goos' becomes irrelevant, because anyone fiddling a little with the experimental conditions and improving the analytical techniques could almost certainly discover in the 'goo' any substance he wanted. What would be more significant would be the unique formation of only a single simple biomolecule, but this has never been demonstrated and almost certainly never will be. [4]

Much more importantly, there is the insurmountable problem of how optically active biomolecules could have been formed in the pre-biotic soup. One cannot envisage any form of life being based on racemic compounds. Proteins are only active because they have secondary and tertiary structures. These structures are only formed when the protein's building blocks, the amino acids, are optically active. Proteins made of racemic amino acids (i.e. L-/D-) would have no activity, in particular, they would have no enzymic activity. And without enzymes there could be no life.

A further difficulty is with the type of amino acid formed in primeval soup experiments. In fact none of the essential protein amino acids are found in the soup. This is surprising when one thinks of the propaganda widely put about. For instance, the aromatic amino acids, tyrosine, tryptophan and phenylalanine have not been discovered in soup experiments. They are, however, essential for the construction of enzymes. In addition, the basic amino acids arginine, histidine and lysine have also not been found in sufficient amounts. Furthermore, the amino acids that are found in soup experiments, for example, β-alanine, sarcosine, diaminopropionic acid etc., are not in fact components of proteins. These amino acids are much more abundant in soup experiments than protein amino acids, like leucine, for instance, so one cannot fail to wonder whether these experiments are on the wrong track altogether. These failures have been glossed over and largely ignored by supporters of the primeval soup notion.

The conclusion from three decades of experimentation on primeval soup models is that small traces of virtually any simple organic compound may be produced. Their presence, however, is of dubious significance because it is simply a measure of the sophisticated analytical procedures used in their detection. If one wants to find a particular molecule it is always possible to do so if one looks long enough and has the highly sensitive techniques necessary for its detection.

On reading many elementary textbooks the reader obtains a grossly false impression of the significance of Miller's experiments. These experiments have not demonstrated the formation of protein amino acids at all! Glycine and racemic alanine are the principal amino acids and one cannot envisage a protein being constructed from just these two amino acids.

Nucleic acid bases have indeed been found. But, the fact is, they are produced in minute quantity. There is absolutely no pathway from these to the complicated nucleotides needed to produce a nucleic acid. Even after three decades of intensive experimentation, 'soup' experiments are no nearer a solution and, contrary to the impression gained from textbooks, the formation of prevital nucleic acids that in any way resemble DNA and RNA is unproven.

The entire primeval soup story is a classic example of how easily science may enter a blind alley and become inextricably lost. Right from the outset the *modus operandi* of scientists working in this field was in error. Even the most junior undergraduate chemist knows all too well that one cannot take arbitrary mixtures of components and hope to end up with a pure product. Such a procedure is a recipe for disaster. Producing 'goos' and tarry messes and then demonstrating one's expertise at chemical analysis might lead to one, or two, publications and accreditation as an analyst *par excellence*, but that is about all. Its value in the search for life's origin is extremely dubious.

Formation of giant biomolecules
If despite the above criticism, we accept the existence of a primeval ocean, containing a large number of small

biomolecules, there next comes the problem how these compounds would have reacted together to give polymers. Proteins are formed when amino acids condense together with the loss of water, and polysaccharides when sugars do so, thus:

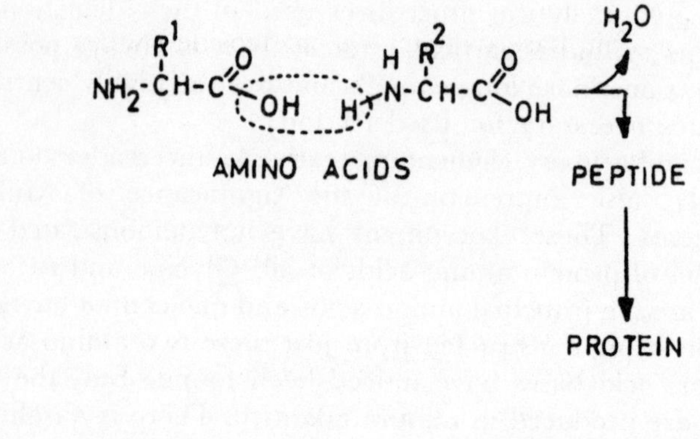

AMINO ACIDS   PEPTIDE

PROTEIN

DISACCHARIDE

POLYSACCHARIDE

One problem must be to account for the loss of water in these reactions for they occur *in* water. It is difficult to lose water from a condensation reaction if it takes place surrounded by water. Of course, reactions like these occur all the time in living cells in an environment of water, but they do so because living organisms are able to give an input of energy needed to drive the reaction to completion. In cells this is normally provided by the molecule ATP and the reaction is further catalysed by specific enzymes. Although ATP might well have been present in the primeval soup, enzymes certainly were not.

In the case of nucleic acids a three-stage process would be required even before the simplest dinucleotide could be formed:

Stage (i)

$$\text{organic base} + \text{sugar} \longrightarrow \text{nucleoside} + \text{water}$$

Stage (ii)

$$\text{nucleoside} + \text{phosphoric acid} \longrightarrow \text{nucleotide} + \text{water}$$

Stage (iii)

$$\text{nucleotide}_1 + \text{nucleotide}_2 \longrightarrow \text{dinucleotide} + \text{water}$$

All of these reactions release water, so the same problems as discussed for the formation of proteins apply. In addition, there are a large number of possible isomers at each stage, so much so that it is difficult to see how a uniform nucleic acid could result. This will be discussed in detail later; at this stage let us consider how any condensation resulting in the loss of water could occur in the primeval soup scenario. Two possible mechanisms have been proposed. The first is that giant biomolecules were formed in locations of relatively high temperature, known to exist, for instance, in the vicinity of volcanoes. These areas would also be relatively anhydrous and would facilitate condensation reactions. The second proposal has been the suggestion that certain natural mineral substances might have acted as catalysts for dehydration condensations.

Formation of proteins

The American biochemist Sidney Fox has studied the products formed when mixtures of amino acids are subjected to such heat as might occur in exposed rocks of a volcanic primeval earth. The products obtained have been named 'protenoids'. These have been found to resemble proteins in that they have high molecular weight and are susceptible to attack by proteolytic enzymes. The amino acid glutamic acid is particularly effective in promoting the formation of protenoids. When protenoids are suspended in warm water and viewed under the microscope a large number of small globules are observed. Fox has claimed that these microspheres resemble what would have been the precursors of cells, so-called 'protocells'. A number of other scientists have gone along with Fox and supported the view that the dry-heat polymerization of amino acids might have been the first stage in the development of primeval life. However, this seems highly unlikely. Firstly, when amino acids are heat-polymerized they lose their optical activity, therefore the resulting protenoids cannot be true resemblances of natural proteins. And secondly, the fact that microspheres are formed when water is added is neither here nor there, as many polymers form similar emulsions when added to water.

Other mechanisms for the formation of proteins have been put forward. One involves the condensation reagent dicyandiamide $[NH_2 C(=NH) N=C=NH]$, a known product of primeval soup experiments. This substance is known to be capable of forming peptides from amino acids; however, in trial experiments only small peptides have been formed. The dry-hot reaction is much more successful in producing large protein-like material.

It is vitally important to draw attention to the fact that these model experiments carried out on the laboratory bear little resemblance to what could have occurred on the primeval earth. The primeval soup, by definition, had to be a complex mix of thousands upon thousands of different molecules. If this soup had dried up on exposed volcanic rocks it is extremely doubtful if amino acids could have polymerized as might be suggested from these simple experiments. The most likely product would have been a horrible tarry 'goo'. Furthermore, although synthetic peptides do indeed fold themselves into configurations resembling natural proteins, this would not have occurred under primeval soup conditions because (i) the peptides formed would have been racemic, and (ii) they would have consisted of *random* sequences of amino acids.

Contrary to much of the published work, which on the whole bears little relevance to the problem, it is highly unlikely that molecules resembling proteins as we know them could have formed spontaneously either on hot exposed volcanic rocks or within the soup itself.

Formation of nucleic acids

Nucleic acids are formed when nucleotides polymerize; nucleotides are therefore a prerequisite. *Nucleotides, however, are not formed under simple primeval soup experiments.* Let us put this aside for the moment and see what difficulties remain. Nucleotides, as has been mentioned previously, consist of a Base + Sugar + Phosphate. The first problem regarding their prebiotic formation is the origin of the phosphate. In watery environments the predominant chemical form of phosphorus is phosphoric acid ($H_3 PO_4$). However, on the primeval earth this would combine with calcium and other alkaline earth metals, so that there would be very little dissolved phosphate in the primordial soup.

The second problem with the spontaneous formation of nucleotides is in the large number of possible isomers that may result when phosphate is added to a nucleoside. Suppose the nucleoside adenosine underwent random condensation with phosphoric acid, the following phosphate esters would result:

adenosine — 3′ — phosphate,
adenosine — 5′ — phosphate,
adenosine — 3′, 5′ — phosphate,
adenosine — 2′, 5′ — phosphate,
adenosine — 2′ — phosphate,
adenosine — 2′, 5′ — phosphate.

Cyril Ponnamperuma, in the United States, has demonstrated that when the nucleoside adenosine is heated with sodium dihydrogen phosphate *in the absence of water* at 160°C, then many of the above isomers are obtained.[5] And Sidney Fox has shown that phosphorylation may occur on the 5′ (OH) group of the nucleoside if the condensing reagent was polyphosphoric acid, a compound that may have existed on the primitive earth, but the number of possible isomers formed during these condensations is extremely large. To suggest further that these monomeric nucleotides, existing in a variety of isomeric forms, could polymerize to give a nucleic acid presents such insurmountable problems as to make it completely implausible.

Nucleotides, in comparison to amino acids, are unstable in aqueous solution. When dissolved in water they tend to break down into their components. Thus even if they were formed in the primeval soup they would not have remained intact for very long. In addition, nucleotides are unstable to ultraviolet light, which would also have led to their demise. One may safely conclude that the primeval earth may have generated a 'soup' of amino acids, but it certainly would not have become a 'soup' of nucleotides.

At best nucleotides may have formed only in specific locations, for instance, on the exposed rocks adjacent to a source of volcanic heat. In such a site one needs to postulate the presence of a high concentration of purine and pyrimidine bases. Sugar molecules present little difficulty as they may readily be formed by the polymerization of formaldehyde (HCHO). Combination of a sugar molecule and a base would result in the formation of a nucleoside. This could have been a dry-phase reaction but considerable problems remain.

Ribose is a pentose sugar which may exist in either an α- or β- form having either a furanose (5-membered) ring, or a pyranose (6-membered) ring. It may also occur as a D- or an L- form. Thus with ribose there are eight different isomers possible, making a grand total of forty-eight different possible isomers for each nucleotide formed. How could such a mixture of nucleotides polymerize to give a uniform polymer?

Dr Cairns-Smith has concluded that the formation of a nucleic acid on the primeval earth is a 'gigantic implausibility'. [6] I would go one step further and say that it is a gigantic impossibility!

If one goes along with the evolutionists, one must believe in the *miraculous* spontaneous formation of nucleic acids in the primeval soup. Accordingly one no longer has a naturalistic explanation for the origin of life.

Summary and conclusion

Let us consider the wildly unlikely happening of an enzyme-like molecule being formed in the primeval soup. The assumption that enzymes were the first giant biomolecules is sound, simply because without them life could not have got started. Let us further suppose that there also existed some miraculous mechanism for their synthesis. Now this miracle would be in vain simply because the environment of the primeval soup would render any enzyme molecule barren. By definition, the primeval soup was a hotch-potch of almost every conceivable chemical. In such a mixture it is inevitable there would have been innumerable enzyme inhibitors or 'poisons'. Accordingly, as soon as an enzyme appeared in the soup its action would have been inhibited.

The same applies to the nucleic acids. Again let us suppose a miraculous mechanism for the formation of DNA. This also would be futile, for it simply could not function because of the presence in the soup of innumerable nucleotide analogues. They would have become incorporated into DNA and so inhibited its role. Nucleotide analogues, or 'anti-metabolites', are well known today as medicines. They are employed to inhibit key stages in cell metabolism. Azauridine, for instance, is used to treat leukaemia and AZT (azathymidine) is now being used in AIDS therapy. It takes little difficulty to imagine such substances jamming up the primitive metabolism before it had properly got started.

Molecules resembling anti-metabolites and enzyme inhibitors would have been abundant in the primeval soup; so how could the first enzymes have been functional! Anyone who has carried out an enzyme reaction in the laboratory knows all too well how easy it is to poison. By definition the primeval soup would have been full to the brim with such poisons and inhibitors. Life simply could not have got off the ground.

Francis Crick has suggested that if an ingenious choice of chemicals were left around sealed in a flask for about a year then some type of life would form spontaneously. This absurd suggestion only reinforces the view that even Nobel Prize winners may sometimes talk like the men of Gotham. [7]

The major problem with the creation of life out of the chaos of the primeval soup is one of thermodynamics. For in any discussion on the origin of life one has to identify the driving force needed to transform disorganized matter into the highly organized structure that occurs in the living state. In the jargon of thermodynamics, the primeval soup is a system of high entropy (entropy being defined as randomness). We appear to live in a universe where entropy is increasing — everything seems to be running downhill. On the other hand, the living state is one of low entropy. Its formation involves therefore an uphill process in which energy is required. [8]

The question remains what could have been the driving force for the spontaneous creation of life? The same problem applies for the formation of the large biomolecules. We know that whenever either a protein, or a nucleic acid, is dissolved in water, it breaks down, or hydrolyses into amino acids or nucleotides respectively. A mixture of amino acids in water does not spontaneously join together to give a protein molecule, neither does a mixture of nucleotides combine to give a nucleic acid. In energetic terms these are uphill reactions in which energy is required.

Even if the above problem were to be solved, there remain two fundamental complications. The first is that life today depends on both nucleic acids and proteins. Nucleic acids require proteins for their formation and proteins require nucleic acids — so which came first? One can be certain that they did not both appear simultaneously. Protein synthesis in living cells requires not only DNA as the information storage repository, but also messenger RNA, ribosomes and transfer RNA. Ribosomes are the site for protein synthesis yet they contain proteins as integral components of their structure. How could the first proteins have been made? It is a classic chicken and egg predicament. One can argue that the first forms of life were based on RNA alone, but this is extremely dubious as no self-replicating RNA molecule has ever been demonstrated in the laboratory. Although Leslie Orgel and his colleagues have done some interesting work on the replication of simple oligonucleotides, no similar work has been achieved with RNA chains with complex sequences. And, of more significance, no one has taken a primeval soup experiment and fished out anything resembling an RNA molecule — never mind something that had even the remotest chance of replicating! One might add that although some types of RNA might have a limited enzymic activity, this could in no way be sophisticated enough to induce replication.

Life based solely upon proteins is also impossible to envisage. In the absence of nucleic acids, how could the information for protein be transferred from one generation to the next? Indeed, no protein has been demonstrated to possess a simple copying mechanism that could have mimicked nucleic acids. This failure strongly implies that proteins could not have adopted this role.

One cannot dispute the possibility that small pools of primeval soup could have formed on the primitive earth, but these would be haphazard mixtures. It is impossible to see how regular biomolecules like proteins and nucleic acids could have formed from such a recipe. Any mechanism that may be conceived of would almost certainly be subject to fouling up by minor components of the soup.

As we have seen in this chapter, a whole industry has been created, with countless scientists all busily engaged in maltreating various chemical mixtures. But how many have sat down and asked, 'What does it all mean?' Dr Cairns-Smith has commented that most scientists have been blind to the difficulties. Indeed he went on to conclude that 'There almost seems to be a conspiracy not to discuss them.'[9] This is a view I would most readily endorse.

One is left wondering why so many scientists have been eager to work in this field. Clearly to some extent it has been an essential exercise necessary to prop up the rather tottering Darwinism theory. For if chemical evolution is shown to be implausible, then biological evolution is highly questionable. Accordingly, it has been imperative for scientists to formulate a mechanism for chemical evolution.

A second possible motivation has been the fact that the primeval soup scenario has provided a fertile field for scientists to gather material for publication. Indeed, sufficient material has been forthcoming for several new journals to be created.

The upshot has been that many scientists have become irrevocably entangled in a mass of meaningless data. Like the man who becomes lost in a dense forest they are seized with panic and strike out in desperation, in one direction after another, in vain trying to find a recognizable landmark. So too with the primeval soup scenario.

When one recalls the optimism created by Miller's experiment in the early 1950s, one is reminded of T. H. Huxley's remark that 'None deceives himself more than he who feels that a miracle is proved fact when it is proved a bare possibility.' [10]

4. The problem of molecular chirality

All life has associated with it chirality, or 'optical activity'. This fact poses a major problem because most chemical reactions normally proceed with no regard to chirality. This being so, why, if life evolved along a spontaneous process from non-living matter, did it acquire chirality? Let us firstly consider what is meant by the term chirality.

Chirality

When an object is not superimposable on its mirror image it is said to be 'chiral'. Chiral structures have associated with them 'handedness'. This is best illustrated if, for example, we take our own hands. If our right hand is placed in front of a mirror we will see an image of a left hand, and vice versa. Although we may put our hands together, as in prayer, when they appear to be identical, it is not possible to superimpose one on top of the other. Try it and see. Now this is what chirality is all about.

Chirality may extend from complicated structures like our hands right down to the molecular level. It is a curious fact that all living organisms employ chiral molecules. The fundamental problem is 'why?' It is only the living state where chirality seems important. Most chemical reactions proceed perfectly normally with little regard to chirality. If the primeval soup theory is true, how did the first forms of life distinguish between different chiral molecules?

Optical activity

All chiral molecules exhibit what is known as optical activity. The discovery of optical activity goes back to the early nineteenth century, when it was found that certain crystalline minerals, such as quartz and Iceland spar, were able to produce plane polarized light. It is not necessary to go into the details of what this is in physical terms. The essentials may be appreciated from a superficial view. Most people have come across 'polarized' sun glasses. Even if they have not actually worn a pair, they have almost certainly seen their effect on reducing light intensity from television advertisements. With these glasses the lenses are made from a special type of plastic that acts like quartz and Iceland spar in permitting only a selected type of light to pass through. A rough analogy is to imagine the crystal, or lens, to be a closed book. This easily permits the insertion of a flat knife between the pages only when the blade of the knife is held in the same plane of the pages of the book. So it is with a beam of light passing through a polarizer.

In 1815 the French physicist Jean Baptiste Biot (1774-1862) discovered that most naturally occurring organic substances are able to rotate the plane of polarized light. These he described as exhibiting 'optical activity'. Some substances were able to rotate it clockwise — these were called 'dextro-rotatory'; others rotated it anti-clockwise, which gave them the name 'laevo-rotatory'.

Optical activity arises in an organic chemical when there are one or more asymmetric carbon atoms. An asymmetric carbon atom is one where there are four different groups attached to it. In the illustration opposite we have the molecular structure of lactic acid and its mirror image:

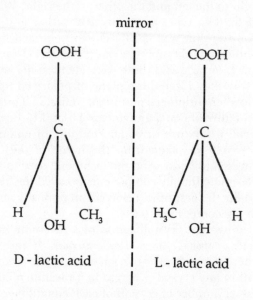

D - lactic acid   L - lactic acid

These two molecules are called 'enantiomers'. On the left is (R) lactic acid, R being derived from the Latin *rectus* meaning right, and (D-) because it is dextro-rotatory. Its mirror image is (S) lactic acid, S from the Latin *Sinister,* being left, and (L-) because it is laevo-rotatory. (D- and L- are the old-fashioned terms and are frequently replaced by (R), (S) in modern textbooks.)

The major advances in the study of optical activity were made by Pasteur. His investigations remain a landmark in this field. He made a crucial study of the different forms of tartaric acid that were obtained from grape juice concentrates. In particular he investigated the substance known as 'racemic acid' (derived from the Latin *racemus,* grape). Racemic acid was a chemical puzzle because it had the same chemical composition as tartaric acid, yet had different physical properties. In particular it was unlike tartaric acid in that it had no optical activity. In 1848 Pasteur discovered that crystallized solutions of racemic acid were made up of two different types of crystal. After carefully separating the two types under the microscope, Pasteur made the remarkable discovery that one rotated the plane of polarized light to the left and the other to the right. When equal amounts of the two types were mixed together and dissolved in water, the solution was indifferent to polarized light. Further work indicated that one type of crystal was D-tartaric acid and the other L-tartaric acid. Both were identical in every respect except the way they rotated the plane of polarized light. They were therefore enantiomers or mirror images. Thus racemic acid was a mixture of equal amounts of D- and L- tartaric acid. Today we call a mixture of equal amounts of enantiomers a 'racemate' — a term taken from the name of the first compound discovered to be so. And the technique used in the separation of a racemate into its components is called the 'resolution'. Pasteur had for the first time 'resolved' an optically active compound into its component parts.

We now know that crystallization of a racemate may either give a *racemic compound,* or a *racemic mixture.* A racemic compound is where the molecules of each enantiomer occur in equal amounts within any crystal, whereas in a racemic mixture there occurs an equal number of crystals of each enantiomer. Pasteur's crystallization of racemic acid resulted in a racemic mixture and this is known as a spontaneous resolution.

Optical activity and life

In 1860 Pasteur reached the profound conclusion that the distinction between inanimate and living matter rested in the optical activity of the molecules of the latter. This was a very perceptive observation, for we now know that the constituents of all living cells are indeed associated with optical activity. Chemical reactions in the laboratory, on the other hand, produce only racemic compounds. Within all living organisms all molecules that are capable of chirality are found in an optically active state. Thus all proteins, nucleic acids and polysaccharides are made up of molecules of uniform chirality. Proteins on hydrolysis always give L-amino acids and nucleic acids D-ribose. Similarly, the hydrolysis of important polysaccharides, such as starch and cellulose, yields D-glucose and never its enantiomer L-glucose.

For many years there raged within the scientific and medical community the contentious issue whether cancer resulted from a loss of chirality within cells. This controversy produced a great deal of speculation but was eventually laid to rest some time at the beginning of this century. (Interestingly, however, it has been discovered during the last decade that during ageing the amino acids in proteins do indeed begin to racemize, but whether this has anything to do with cancer is not known.) [1]

The fact that we do not have in nature two types of organism, one being the mirror image of the other, is strong evidence against the spontaneous evolution of life. What we find is that all organisms are composed of molecules retaining the one kind of chirality. The fundamental riddle is how in the first place could an evolving system distinguish between different chiral molecules. It becomes a problem of discovering the nature of chiral discrimination.

Let us illustrate this by taking the example of the laboratory synthesis of an amino acid. What one ends up with is a mixture of equal quantities of L- and D- isomer, a racemate in other words. In the living cell, however, only the L-amino acid is produced. Such a situation implies that the molecules taking part in the production of the amino acid in the living cell must themselves be chiral.

Problem of universal chirality

The property of optical activity is taken to be associated uniquely with molecules isolated from living organisms. For instance, the discovery of optically active organic molecules in crude oil has been taken as evidence that petroleum has a biological origin.

All biological molecules are organic in that they are based on carbon atoms. As carbon atoms are able to bond with up to four different groups they form asymmetric molecules that result in optical activity. Organic molecules synthesized in the laboratory are always racemic, whereas in natural sources they occur in an optically active form. The importance of this fact becomes evident when one considers the construction of large biomolecules. Enzymes, for instance, are proteins that depend precisely on their three-dimensional structure for activity. Thus a protein made up of racemic amino acids could not adopt a specific shape and so could have no biological activity. Furthermore, a random mixture of L- and D- amino acids in an enzyme molecule also could have no activity. Without chiral uniformity a protein molecule would be unable to fold in the same way twice. Thus it could not be relied upon to have any enzymic activity. Similarly, the double-stranded helical structure of DNA demands its sugar components to have definite shape. If its sugar, deoxyribose, lacked optical activity then the double helix could not form. One may safely conclude that only a chirally uniform nucleic acid could be functional.

The origin of molecular chirality in chemical evolution is of major importance. In an attempt to explain it evolutionists have proposed two possible scenarios:

1. The primeval soup gave rise to only one type of chiral molecule, for example only L-amino acids were formed.

2. Racemic mixtures were indeed produced in the soup but at some stage in the work-up only molecules of a uniform chirality were processed.

The importance of this problem cannot be over-emphasized. If we take, for example, the Miller experiment, this produced only racemic mixtures of amino acids. Life is inconceivable based on such racemates. Therefore, how did life get started? And how did only one of the enantiomers get selected? What we are seeking is a mechanism for chiral discrimination. Let us consider a hypothetical analogy, namely that of a bicycle factory supplied with components for making both D-bicycles and their mirror image L-bicycles. If all the components are randomly mixed-up workers on the production line, after a considerable amount of messing around, would begin assembling. Both L- and D- bicycles could be produced. Alternatively, the line would become clogged-up if workers attempted to construct the useless racemic bicycle. Overall it would be a very inefficient assembly line. A much more efficient factory would employ a group of workers ahead of the production line checking and allowing through only components for one type of bicycle. This process of chiral discrimination would be essential for success.

The same applies to the natural world. Proteins, enzymes and nucleic acids if constructed of molecules of confused chirality would be unable to function and be as useless as a racemic bicycle. What could have been the mechanism for chiral discrimination in the primeval soup scenario? But here we reach an impasse, for chiral discrimination requires some form of original chirality. We reach a classic chicken and egg situation. The question of chiral discrimination is therefore one of the most fundamental problems associated with the origin of life.

Of greater difficulty is the philosophical question as to why life should be based on optically active molecules at all. One can say that as life is based on carbon then chirality inevitably follows. But this evades the central issue, namely, if racemic molecules were generated in the primeval soup, why was it not possible for a form of life to develop based on these? It could be argued that indeed it did and that the first form of life was racemic life and that it was subsequently taken over by optically active life. Yet as has been pointed out above, racemic proteins and nucleic acids could have had no activity. It is inconceivable that life could have developed without regard to chirality.

To suppose that the first forms of life did indeed employ optically active molecules, then one must presuppose a discrimination mechanism. What could this have been? There has been no shortage of suggestions, let us consider some of them.

Mechanisms for stereoselection

1. Spontaneous resolution

In the crystallization of a racemate from a super-saturated solution there may occur the chance and spontaneous crystallization of a pure enantiomer. This is a very, very rare occurrence but it does occasionally happen. Could it have done so in the primeval soup? This is extremely doubtful; for one thing, the solutions would have needed to have been completely free of other substances. This is not the situation with the primeval soup, where the amino acids were very minor constituents. The primeval soup could never have become supersaturated in any particular amino acid excepting glycine, which happens to be the only amino acid that lacks optical activity! Furthermore, no Miller-type experiment has ever been able to produce even a racemic crystalline product, never mind an optically active one.

2. Preferential interaction with radiation

A number of researchers have pursued the idea that certain types of radiation are able to destroy one of a pair of enantiomers. This preferential destruction could lead to an accumulation of one enantiomer in the primeval soup. Circularly polarized sunlight, for example, leads to a selective photochemical decomposition of chiral molecules. The effect is rather weak and it is doubtful whether it could have affected the composition of a primeval soup.

Bremsstrahlung radiation generated when polarized beta rays interact with matter has been found to destroy the enantiomers of amino acids at slightly different rates. [2] Again the effect is weak and therefore seems unlikely to produce a significant effect. Radiation from cobalt-60 has also been found to decompose D-tyrosine more rapidly than L-tyrosine. [3] The effect is again very weak and exposure over several years is needed to get a noticeable effect. Also during exposure to this radiation much of the original racemic mixture is itself destroyed making the whole concept very unlikely.

3. Interaction with chiral surfaces

Probably the most reasonable explanation for chiral discrimination has been the idea that chiral mineral surfaces may have played an important role. For example, one could imagine that stereoselective polymerization of amino acids could occur on kaolinite, or bentonite surfaces. Alternatively there could have been stereoselective adsorption to chiral crystalline minerals, such as quartz, or Iceland spar. Unfortunately there is no laboratory support for these ideas.

4. Chemical dissimilarities of enantiomers

A final hypothesis, and rather more fundamental, is to challenge the widely held concept that enantiomers do indeed have identical physical and chemical properties. One need not postulate a large difference — only minor differences that may have, so far, escaped observation in the laboratory. As yet there is no laboratory evidence for this suggestion. Theoretical calculations have been done on the energy difference between a chiral molecule and its mirror image which do indicate that maybe minute differences do exist. However, the significance of these is doubtful.

Summary

In summary therefore, did the first forms of life use racemic molecules and was this followed by a selection of molecular chirality to give a more efficient evolutionary mechanism? Alternatively did the first forms of life employ optically active molecules? If so, how did these molecules originate? Is life responsible for optical activity, or is optical activity responsible for life? There is so far no answer to this riddle.

Although as we have seen in this chapter the origin of optical activity in living cells must have needed some machinery for chiral discrimination, it must have been available right at the very beginning of life. After many decades of research, evolutionists have concluded that instead of them getting closer to solving this mystery the more elusive it becomes. The more intensely an answer is sought, the more the problem appears to be insoluble. None of the mechanisms proposed above can offer a glimmer of hope; consequently many researchers have thrown up their arms in despair. I believe there is a solution to this dilemma but it does not involve a gradual chemical evolution of life, as we shall discover in the final chapter.

5. *Origin of the genetic code*

The genetic material in all organisms is nucleic acid. It is the nucleic acid that carries the information for protein synthesis. Proteins, as we have seen previously, are able to perform a wide variety of functions within the cell, but are unable to carry genetic information. This is the sole role of nucleic acid.

Nucleic acids consist of polymers of four bases, cytosine (C), guanine (G), adenine (A) and either uracil (U) in RNA, or thymine (T) in DNA. Proteins, on the other hand, are much smaller molecules built up of twenty different amino acids. The DNA of the cell contains all the recipes for the manufacture of every protein needed by that cell. These recipes reside in the arrangement, or sequence of the bases.

In order to translate from the nucleic acid 'language' to that of proteins there exists a 'dictionary' relating the language of bases to that of amino acids. This dictionary is known as the genetic code. The deciphering of this code was accomplished in the early 1960s. It proceeded in the following manner: let us suppose one base coded for one amino acid, for example U could code for the amino acid alanine, and G for glycine and so on. Such a system was quickly ruled out simply because with only four bases there could be no more than four different amino acids in proteins and this was known not to be so. Let us go one step further: suppose units of two bases coded for each amino acid. The number of possible combinations of four bases is now 4^2 i.e. $4 \times 4 = 16$. This implies a total of sixteen different code words and is near to the number of different amino acids found in proteins. It was, however, ruled out from experimental observations using principally the protein-synthesizing machinery of the bacterium *Escherichia coli*. It was clearly demonstrated in this work that in fact three bases coded for each amino acid. Combinations of four bases would now give 4^3 i.e. $4 \times 4 \times 4 = 64$ different possible combinations. This immediately indicated that the genetic code must be 'degenerate', meaning that as only twenty amino acids were in fact incorporated into protein then most must have more than one code word. The code words are referred to as 'codons'. Intensive work has led to the elucidation of the codons for each amino acid. These are shown in Table 1. Subsequent work has led scientists to the conclusion that the genetic code is universal throughout the whole of nature and this universality has been taken as evidence that all species have descended from one common ancestor. It ought to be pointed out that this statement is more one of opinion than of concrete scientific fact. It has been assumed. No one has actually studied the genetic code in a large number of different organisms and shown it to be universal. For one thing, who in their right mind would spend a large part of their life proving the genetic code to be universal when at the end of the day everyone would turn around and say, 'I told you so'? Furthermore who would fund such a project? And would any scientific journal publish it? Francis Crick holds a similar view and has written, 'Since it is suspected that the code will always be the same, few people are keen to spend time on the problem.'[1]

Mechanism of translation

DNA is more stable than RNA, so it is the DNA, contained within the nucleus of the cell, that is the repository for all the genetic information. This DNA is programmed to release short lengths copied on to RNA, and it is these RNA molecules that carry the information from the cell nucleus into the cytoplasm. It is here where the protein-building factories, the so-called ribosomes, exist. The small transcripts of DNA are known as 'messenger' RNA. Messenger RNA (mRNA) molecules have a transient existence, just long enough to produce sufficient of the protein required. During synthesis of this protein the information coded in the mRNA is 'translated' from the nucleic acid language into that of protein. To accomplish this another set of RNA molecules are required. These are called 'transfer'

Number of amino acids in each group	AMINO ACID	Codons					
3	Serine	UCU	UCC	UCA	UCG	AGU	AGC
	Leucine	UUA	UUG	CUU	CUC	CUA	CUG
	Arginine	CGU	CGC	CGA	CGG	AGA	AGG
5	Glycine	GGU	GGC	GGA	GGG		
	Alanine	GCU	GCC	GCA	GCG		
	Valine	GUU	GUC	GUA	GUG		
	Threonine	ACU	ACC	ACA	ACG		
	Proline	CCU	CCC	CCA	CCG		
1	Isoleucine	AUU	AUC	AUA			
9	Phenylalanine	UUU	UUC				
	Tyrosine	UAU	UAC				
	Cysteine	UGU	UGC				
	Histidine	CAU	CAC				
	Glutamine	CAA	CAG				
	Asparagine	AAU	AAC				
	Lysine	AAA	AAG				
	Aspartic acid	GAU	GAC				
	Glutamic acid	GAA	GAG				
2	Trytophan	UGG					
	Methionine	AUG					

TABLE 1

RNAs and their function is to carry specific amino acids directly to the protein factory. In order for them to do this, each one needs a matching enzyme which tags on the specific amino acid.

Thus we have in each protein factory a messenger RNA along which complex ribosomes read off the coded message and simultaneously knit together a string of amino acids. The amino acids are carried to the ribosome on the backs of transfer RNAs. Also coded in the mRNA molecule are certain words that tell the ribosomes to stop building. Another one instructs the ribosome to release the completed chain of amino acids. On release the polypeptide chain folds up into a unique shape which is determined by the order of amino acids. In many ways the protein-synthesizing mechanism, even in the most humble microbe, is akin to the most sophisticated robotic car assembly line imaginable. It is so complex, the great mystery is how did it originate? Could it have evolved from simpler systems? The evolutionist would say it had. But if so, why are all living organisms today based on the same system? If it had developed in stages, one would expect less sophisticated systems to exist as well. But there aren't any. If we follow up the car assembly line analogy, we know that if we inspected car factories throughout the world today we would find a vast spectrum of production lines, from the ones producing hand-built models right up to the fully robotic assembly plant. But in the natural world we simply do not find such a graduation.

Here we come up against another great paradox in the quest for the origin of life. Proteins, as we have seen, are constructed from the information stored in nucleic acids. Nucleic acids, however, cannot begin to make proteins without the existence of proteins in the first place. Nucleic acids themselves cannot exist without the proteins needed for their replication. Proteins require nucleic acids and nucleic acids require proteins. So which came first?

To take the car factory analogy again, let us imagine that the robots on the assembly line resemble the proteins of the cell and that the computer software, that controls the robots, is analogous to the nucleic acids of the cell. A factory without robots and having just the computer software couldn't produce anything and vice versa. The robots and the computer software are both integral parts of the factory. And so it is with

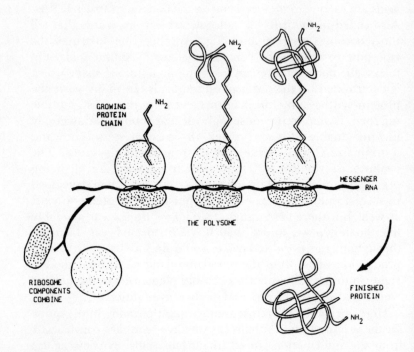

FIGURE 6

Simplified representation of the mechanism for protein biosynthesis.

the living cell, which requires both proteins and nucleic acids. Life is no more possible without proteins and nucleic acids than a modern car assembly line without either computer software or robots.

Origin of the genetic code

In protein assembly each word on the mRNA chain is recognized by a smaller tRNA molecule that is able to bind to it. Thus if the code word is UUU then a tRNA carrying the amino acid phenylalanine attaches itself to that position. The phenylalanine is then transferred to the growing peptide chain. Each of the original code words is referred to as a 'codon' and its matching partner on the tRNA as an 'anti-codon'.

Amino acids themselves seem to have little ability to combine to their specific codons, so it is extremely difficult to conceive how this process ever got started. How on earth could the coding arrangement have originated? One thing that is immediately obvious if we look at Table 1 is that similar amino acids have similar codons. Look at the two acids, glutamic acid and aspartic acid. Both are coded for by the codon GAX where X is either A or G for glutamic acid, and for aspartic acid either U or C. One might take this as evidence that the genetic code has developed from a simpler code in which GA(?) alone coded for either of the acids, and that during evolution it became refined. Did the genetic code originate then as a triplet code at the outset, with only the first two bases essential? Such a genetic code would imply considerable ambiguity, thus there could have been no discrimination between glutamic acid (GAA) and aspartic acid (GAU), nor between histidine (CAU) and glutamine (CAA), and so on. It could work for the two acids, for one might imagine little disruption in protein structure if one became substituted by the other. If, on the other hand, one were to consider the substitution of lysine (AAA) for asparagine (AAU) this would be completely different and one would expect different properties for the protein produced. It simply would not work. Lysine and asparagine are so different that it is inconceivable they could be interchanged without drastic effects. The same applies for substituting histidine (CAU) with glutamine (CAA). The genetic code could not therefore have originated in this way.

A second possibility is that the genetic code evolved from a triplet code from the very beginning but that only the middle letter actually coded for the particular amino acid. For example, the codon (-U-) would code for leucine (UUA), methionine (AUG), isoleucine (AUU), phenylalanine (UUU) and valine (GUA). These are in fact all similar amino acids and are known as 'hydrophobic'. This type of amino acid plays a vital role in giving essential structural features to a protein and it is not outside the bounds of possibility that members of this group could be interchanged without too drastic an effect on protein structure. Although it would work well for this group of amino acids, it is not as straightforward for others. Proline, for instance, is coded for by CCU, if the middle letter only carried the information, i.e. (-C-), this would also recognize alanine (GCU), serine (UCU) and threonine (ACG). As proline is essential in protein structure, for it allows the polypeptide chain to fold up correctly, it just could not be replaced by either alanine, serine or threonine. It seems implausible therefore that the genetic code originated as a triplet code and was then improved on. The only possibility we are left with is that the genetic code developed in stages. In the beginning just one base coded for a particular type of amino acid and this was followed by a code containing two bases, finally being refined to the present system where three bases code for a unique amino acid.

At the outset it ought to be made clear that this route is least favoured by the majority of scientists who have investigated this problem. What sort of life could have been possible with a one-base genetic code? It must have been remarkably simple. To step up to a system having a doublet code would have been a major advance with very much more sophisticated proteins being possible. Some versatility would have existed and one could see that mutation followed by natural selection might have operated. The intermediate stages, however, are problematical. Let us take specific examples.

Suppose in the most primitive scenario where we have a life form in which the four bases A, G, C and U coded for, let us say, the amino acids aspartic acid, glycine, cysteine and leucine. One could imagine a useful collection of proteins being made from these four amino acids. But what happens when the changeover to a doublet code occurs? Suppose a mutant organism develops able to incorporate the amino acid arginine from the doublet code CG. Accordingly an original stretch of nucleic acid of sequence -UACGUA- instead of coding for the peptide sequence -Leu.Asp.Cys.Gly.Leu.Asp- would now code for -Leu.Asp.Arg.Leu.Asp.- This might have certain advantages and one could argue that natural selection could take over. But the problem is this: in the early stages mixtures of products would result, with arginine in some places and cysteine-glycine in others. This simply would not be a more efficient set-up than was initially present. If natural selection operated it would be quickly eliminated. It is therefore inconceivable that a life form could operate when two different genetic codes were present. This is even more so when one goes one step further and postulates going from a doublet code to a triplet code. Life based on a doublet code could indeed produce a sophisticated array of proteins, but during the switch to a triplet code there would be utter chaos. The whole idea is just implausible.

The major problem with the evolution of a genetic code is that the first forms of life must have been able to produce proteins before the existence of a code. The alternative is to suppose a form of life based entirely on RNA. Some scientists believe that this might have been possible. I disagree entirely. Although some RNA molecules have been found to have enzyme-like activity, the so-called 'ribozymes', they would have been unlikely to have maintained the variety of chemical reactions necessary for metabolism as we know it. One should think of nucleic acids as informational molecules and liken them to computer software. The hardware, the computers themselves, are dependent on the software, and in living cells are analogous to the proteins. Life with only nucleic acids would be like having computer programmes but no computers.

It is difficult to envisage organisms without a genetic code and it is equally difficult to see how our present genetic code could have evolved from a simpler system. There aren't any organisms today that employ a doublet genetic code, for instance. If they had existed at some time in the past, why have they become extinct? One is led to the inevitable conclusion that the genetic code must have arisen *in toto* at a single stroke. The importance of this conclusion will be developed further in the final chapter where it will be seen to provide scientific support for special creation.

6. *Genetic takeover*

It is an old tradition in science that when you want to breathe
new life into an unsuccessful theory then you must make it
more complicated. The theory described in this chapter known
as 'genetic takeover' is a classic example of this tradition. The
theory itself, like many others in the history of science, was
literally dreamed up about twenty years ago by Dr Graham
Cairns-Smith, a lecturer in chemistry at the University of
Glasgow. In an interview with the magazine *Chemistry in Britain*
in 1982 Dr Cairns-Smith recalled once reading Oparin's *Origin
of Life* as a bedside book. 'What that did for me', he is reported
as saying, 'was to make me see that this was a problem that
you really could think about sensibly. It wasn't just science
fiction.'[1] Soon afterwards the theory of genetic takeover was
revealed to him like a prophetic dream of old. The strange fact
is that it had all been foretold by N. W. Pirie, who had written
some time in the early 1970s: 'Perhaps someone will write a
book explaining the irrelevance of both nucleic acids and proteins
and attributing our existence to the interactions of hydrocarbons and silica.'[2]

My pillory of Dr Cairns-Smith is justified because his theory
has thrown a blanket of scientific obscurantism over the problem
of the origin of life. To appreciate its finer points one needs
at least an honours degree in chemistry and the danger is that
the theory will become over-simplified and incorporated into
conventional wisdom with few people actually understanding
the essential details. Yet I do credit him with one thing and
that is that he has been the first British scientist to come out
and openly declare the implausibility of the primeval soup
hypothesis.

In his theory Dr Cairns-Smith postulates that two forms of life have existed on our earth. One is our own form of life; the second is a primary life form, a sort of 'starter life', or 'proto-life'. The doctor is fond of using the trendy analogy of a type of 'low tech' life being superseded by a 'high tech' variety. The theory is propounded at considerable length in two books, *Genetic Takeover* (1982) and *Seven Clues to the Origin of Life* (1985). The latter work treats the origin of life as a mystery requiring a Sherlock Holmes solution.

According to Cairns-Smith's theory the primary life form was based on the microcrystals of clay minerals. The idea develops the old analogy between the living state and crystallization that was first discussed by Kant. In *Seven Clues to the Origin of Life* he describes how a supersaturated solution of photographer's hypo may be seeded by adding a couple of crystals, then 'Watch amazed at what happens'. Probably a better illustration is that of the chemical 'garden' often made by children with a simple chemistry set. Most people have seen one of these prepared by adding a few crystals of copper sulphate to water glass. Fascinating crystal structures grow just like real plants — but is it really a satisfactory parallel of life? Hasn't it all got to be taken with a pinch of salt?

Crystals as information stores

If one looks at the crystals in a sugar bowl one will find that they all have approximately the same size. It is normally very difficult to grow large crystals because what one usually finds is that when crystals reach a particular size they break up.

Crystal growth occurs by successive surface nucleation. During this process errors may occur. These may be divided into the following categories:

(i)   atoms may be missing at particular sites — i.e. vacancies;

(ii) wrong atoms may be inserted — i.e. substitutions;

(iii) complete rows of atoms may be out of alignment — i.e. dislocations.

(iv) There might occur stacking faults.

If many mistakes occur then the crystal formed may be less stable, i.e. more soluble, than a perfect crystal. It therefore dissolves. That particular pattern of crystal is therefore eliminated for only the more stable ones will continue to spread throughout the solution. It is theoretically, at least, a sort of natural selection.

Cairns-Smith has likened crystal growth to DNA replication in which there is an inherent proof-reading mechanism which controls the product. The crystals Cairns-Smith has postulated as being the primary form of life are the microcrystals of clay. Clay minerals were chosen because of their abundance and their structural versatility. Before we go on to look at the theory in detail we need to appreciate just what clays are.

What are clays?

Despite their appearances mud and clay are highly structured materials. Clays are usually defined as microcrystalline materials that form from water flowing over rocks on the earth's surface. Although their origin is relatively complicated this simple view of them forming by the weathering of rocks will suffice. Thus over long periods of time rocks become worn down by rain and frost, the fragments eventually being carried away to rivers and streams and becoming deposited in sediments as clays. The most abundant weathering product of granite is kaolinite, which is the commonest clay. Kaolinite has the formula $Al_4[Si_4O_{10}]$ $(OH)_8$ and is the major constituent of china clay (kaolin). It has a crystal structure of multiple molecular layers stacked on top of each other.

Serpentine clays have the general formual $Mg_3[Si_2O_5]$ $(OH)_4$. The best known is chrysotile or white asbestos. This exists as a layered structure which is rolled-up in swiss-roll fashion giving it a silky fibrous appearance. Micas are ubiquitous clays and are found in both igneous and metamorphic rocks and sediments. A typical example is muscovite $K\ Al_2\ [Si_3Al\ O_{10}]$ $(OH,F)_2$. A final type of clay, and one which most people are familiar with is talc, which has the formula $Mg_3[Si_4O_{10}](OH)_2$.

Vital clays

The microcrystals in a mineral clay might, with a stretch of the imagination, serve as primitive genetic material in a mineral-based form of life. This would involve within the silicate lattice an irregular distribution of metal ions (for example, Al^{3+}, and Mg^{2+}) carrying information, just as the bases in a nucleic acid do so in life today. If some of these patterns favour a certain crystal size, or shape, then these particular defects would become more common. Let us take as an example a microcrystalline clay within a sandstone rock. If the microcrystals are too small they will simply be washed away; if on the other hand they clog up the rock pores, then water containing material for their growth would be diverted so they would stop their development. The most successful microcrystal is the one that allows water to flow but is large enough for it not to be dislodged. These crystals would therefore be the ones most propagated. Thus we have the scenario in which clay crystals are perpetuating themselves in rock crevices and multiplying by periodic shedding of 'seeds' to adjacent sites.

The next stage involves the production of 'vital muds', that is, assemblages of genetic and non-genetic clays. These clays would have developed some degree of control. Complexes will have been formed enabling certain synthesis to continue and specific propagation. It is postulated that these vital muds would have formed below the ground maybe at the bottom of the seas. This is the low-tech 'life' envisaged by Dr Cairns-Smith. It would not have been a cellular form of life as we know it today. It would have consisted of an interlocking conglomerate of clays with associated other minerals such as zeolites and metal oxides. These 'living organisms' would not have been tiny structures as today's cells are. The good doctor has estimated they may have been several metres in dimension. They are deemed 'alive' because in a sense they could change their behaviour and properties to aid their survival in a changed environment. Reproduction would be slow, however. Dr Cairns-Smith has speculated that it might take a hundred years for just one organism to reproduce — one wonders how he arrived at this estimate.

The flat surfaces of the microcrystals might have been able to catalyse particular chemical reactions. There is indeed considerable evidence that this is possible. Aharon Katchalsky of the Weizmann Institute in Israel has shown that clays will promote the polymerization of amino acids to form protein-like chains, provided there is a source of energy. At this stage in the evolution of life, organic molecules formed by pre-biotic synthesis may have had a significant effect on the physical properties of the clay. We know, for instance, that certain organic molecules, such as the tannins, have dramatic effects on the rheological properties of clay. For this reason they are frequently employed to lubricate parts when drilling through mud. Presumably the mechanism is for the organic molecules to neutralize electrical charges on the clay, so breaking up molecular bonding and making it easier for layers to slip over each other. Thus a firm lump of clay may be made to liquefy by treating it with a simple organic substnce. Furthermore, organic molecules may act as catalysts for clay synthesis. Oxalate, for example, because it is able to chelate aluminium ions encourages the synthesis of kaolinite clays. Organic substances may therefore be beneficial to certain clays, and a form of natural selection may have stepped in.

Once organic molecules arrived on the scene the possibilities became unlimited. Those clays on the surface, for instance, may have taken advantage of the sunlight leading to the beginnings of photosynthesis. Simple metabolic pathways may have commenced leading to the multistep synthesis of complex organic molecules. In particular the biosynthesis of important chiral molecules may eventually have been achieved. Nucleotides may have been synthesized and then the first proto-nucleic acids. These would have been able to self-replicate, so a new secondary genetic material would have arrived on the scene.

Following the synthesis of the first organic genes a symbiotic relationship will have developed between the organic and inorganic genes. Cairns-Smith has called these organisms 'heterogenetic' because they employed two types of genetic material. At some stage the secondary genetic material would have proved more efficient and versatile, particularly following the 'invention' of proteins. Consequently the secondary genetic machinery would have begun to control key steps in the life cycle of the primary, or low-tech organism.

In the final stage the clay material is dispensed with entirely and the high-tech organism took off. To use Dr Cairns-Smith's metaphor: 'The initial booster rocket fell away.'

Evidence for genetic takeover

When at an extraordinary Royal Society conference in May 1974, Dr Cairns-Smith was asked the question: 'Will life be recreated on the laboratory bench?' he replied, 'Yes — a very simple form of life . . .' Such rashness ill becomes a scientist, for the idea that life, of any form, could be created in the laboratory is talking through one's hat. If not, why after more than a dozen years, hasn't Dr Cairns-Smith, or someone else, taken some clays and cooked them up with an appropriate assortment of organic molecules to create a clay monster? Maybe he has and hasn't told us, but I doubt it! One has to admit that clay synthesis of any kind is not easy research, so maybe it's too much to expect. However, what should be possible is for the supporters of this theory to demonstrate any of the following:

(i) The existence of clay organisms today. Dr Cairns-Smith is rather ambiguous about this, for he is on record as saying clay-life is (maybe) going on around us and we just haven't come across it. At the same time he has claimed that present-day microbes have eaten up all trace of them. Either way it is just not good enough. After twenty years one would have thought he would have found it by now. One is curious to know how he would recognize it, however.

(ii) Fossil evidence for clay organisms.

(iii) Failing (i) and (ii), it should be possible to show an active interaction between organic molecules and clay minerals. For instance, many tannin-like organic molecules exist in the environment, but do they exist in symbiotic relationship to clays today?

(iv) It should be possible to demonstrate natural selection processes taking place in clays today.

None of these has so far been demonstrated. The most important is the failure to demonstrate clay-based organisms today. Simply to state that they are extinct is not good enough. Furthermore, to argue that microbes have destroyed them is not satisfactory because how could life based on organic genes destroy a mineral-based life?

Ten doubts

1. The theory fails to explain its very title. How did secondary life 'take over' from primary life? This is the most obscure and inconsistent aspect of the theory.

2. Today we can see clays in abundance in the environment and all around them there are organisms like ourselves made up of organic genes. But nowhere is there anything in between. Where is the intermediate form of life between clays and organic life? If the doctor is right, there were heterogenetic organisms some time in the past — where are they today?

3. The theory fails to explain how genetic information may have been transferred from inorganic minerals to nucleic acids. It is difficult to conceive how information may have been transferred from one to the other. Dr Cairns-Smith likes to use glib analogies such as low technology and high technology — the bow and arrow and the machine gun and so on. These seemingly appealing metaphors are both unrealistic and deceptive.

4. The theory doesn't really solve anything — it's just a wild goose chase. All the problems inherent to the Oparin-Haldane theory all remain. One still has to explain the mechanism for chiral discrimination, the synthesis of nucleic acids and the origin of the genetic code. One is left wondering why the theory was proposed in the first place.

5. By definition, according to this theory, life as we know it could only have originated in specific and rare clay localities; this makes the spontaneous formation of it *less* likely. Instead of having a primeval soup scenario involving an infinite number of 'pools' across the globe, we now have only a finite number of locations.

6. If secondary life did develop from a precursor then it must have done so using those intermediates provided by the primary life. So how could it have escaped and eventually become independent? It is all very well to speculate but genetic takeover is a last resort hypothesis. There is absolutely no experimental evidence to support it. It is looking at the problem through rose-coloured glasses.

7. The idea of heterogenetic organisms is simply implausible. Any organism employing both organic and inorganic genes would be hopelessly inefficient. Indeed, if natural selection were to be involved one would expect these organisms to be the first to be eliminated. Using Dr Cairns-Smith's analogy, one would not expect a factory making bows and arrows to become more efficient if it suddenly switched to making machine guns as well. One needs to look at the car industry to appreciate the truth of this.

8. The whole suggestion that there was a primary life, or 'proto-life', creates unnecessary difficulties. One may immediately smell a rat, for it now becomes necessary to formulate two theories: the first explaining how proto-life formed and then a second explaining how our present life developed. Genetic takeover has all the hallmarks of an altogether bad theory.

9. Next comes the problem of reproduction in clay-based life. How could a parent mineral organism divide to produce two daughter organisms? In particular how could each daughter become detached from the parent and assume an independent existence?

10. Finally, the theory of genetic takeover is unnecessarily complicated. To comprehend it properly one needs to appreciate the finer complexities of crystal growth and the subtleties of difficult silicate chemistry. Yet the overall concept is deceptively simple. The inevitable consequence will be for people to assume the theory and leave aside the complex chemical argument. Unfortunately this is beginning to happen and the theory is being taught to schoolchildren. Will it soon be incorporated into the textbooks and made to appear as if it were a fact, as was done with the primeval soup theory? All this is well illustrated in a letter published last year in the *Daily Telegraph,*

following one I had published drawing attention to the inadequacy of the primeval soup theory:

> 'Sir — For a lecturer in biology L. R. Croft seems remarkably ignorant of some of the more recent advances in our understanding of the origins of life . . . Dr A. G. Cairns-Smith of Glasgow University has put forward a very convincing argument that the first life was probably inorganic and crystalline in nature . . .'[3]

Conclusions

The actual publication of the theory of genetic takeover serves to highlight the fact that the quest for the origin of life is now floundering in a Slough of Despond. Cairns-Smith himself has acknowledged the fact that the idea was only created simply because all other theories are grossly inadequate. He writes, 'Now there might be no need to postulate an earlier kind of life if some minimum-protein system could be conceived of as having formed spontaneously on the primitive Earth. *But I do not see such a system as conceivable.*'[4] And again, *'I see no alternative to postulating some other kind of starter life* to provide the milieu within which our kind of life system began its evolution.'[5]

In other words, as the spontaneous formation of life is now seen to be scientifically implausible one is forced to seek an alternative — any alternative, that is, except special creation. Cairns-Smith completely acknowledges that the primeval soup theory, panspermia and so on are all inadequate. Indeed he goes further and speculates that there seems to be a conspiracy not to discuss their failures. He is one of the few scientists to speak his mind about this. Yet, forced into a corner, he has refused to see special creation as a scientific alternative to his theory of clay.

The tragedy will be if genetic takeover becomes accepted simply because there is no plausible alternative. Indeed, there are signs of this happening today as the letter to the *Daily Telegraph* quoted above confirms. Furthermore, the theory has been boosted by Dr Richard Dawkins, who describes it at length

in his latest book *The Blind Watchmaker;* Dr Dawkins takes it
to the ultimate absurdity by asking whether we in turn will
be taken over by intelligent computers. He writes, 'Will a robotic
Cairns-Smith write a book called *Electronic Takeover?*' And 'Will
one of them tumble to the heretical truth that they have sprung
from a remote, earlier form of life, rooted in organic carbon
chemistry, rather than the silicon-based electronic principles
of their own bodies?'[6]

Scientists like Dawkins and Cairns-Smith have become
entombed in a web of their own conceit. We need not similarly
become entrapped for there is a solution to the problem, as
we will see in the final chapter.

7. Molecules to cells?

Looking at the biochemistry of living organisms today we see that it is a dialogue between two classes of molecule. There are the nucleic acids, which may be seen to be the cell's administrators, and then there are the executive class of molecule, namely the proteins. Proteins are infinitely versatile and go to make up the structure of living things. Some have specific catalytic activity and are known as enzymes. These control the metabolic processes within the cell. Even within the simplest cell it is estimated that there are, at least, 2000 different chemical reactions occurring simultaneously to give an interlocking circuitry which we call life. Every one of those 2000 reactions is precisely controlled by an enzyme molecule.

As we have briefly reviewed in a previous chapter, within the cell there is a division of labour among the nucleic acid molecules. On the one hand the DNA contains the master code for life, whereas the RNA acts as a class of molecule responsible for carrying out instructions passed on from DNA. The essential operations in the biology of a cell may be outlined as follows:

DNA $\longrightarrow$ RNA $\longrightarrow$ Protein
　　　Transcription　　　Translation

Replication

Thus the copying of the message in the master code (the DNA) is known as 'replication'. When the information is transferred from DNA to RNA the process is known as 'transcription'. And when the information coded for in the sequences of bases in the RNA is turned into the amino acid sequences of proteins it is known as 'translation'.

The processes of replication, transcription and translation take place at extremely high speed. What is miraculous is that they involve amazingly few errors. Take for instance, replication: here the error rate is estimated to be about one in 100,000,000 bases. This far exceeds what any modern computer could achieve. How is it accomplished? More pertinently, how could such a process have arisen by blind chance?

The accomplishment of such high fidelity is brought about by the involvement of an intrinsic battery of enzymes that continuously proof-read the processes. If any errors are discovered they are corrected and the process continues. The replication of DNA may be compared to the construction of a hundred-storey high skyscraper, accomplished in *three hours,* with no door, window or door handle in the wrong place!

At the molecular level, replication is achieved by a process of specific molecular recognition and self-correction. At every step in the process of replication, as also in translation and transcription, specific enzymes and proteins are working in unison; just as in the skyscraper analogy a veritable army of construction workers would have had to work quickly and smoothly together.

Even in the simplest known cell all these processes occur with the same precision and complexity. The materialist would have us believe that such organization developed gradually from inanimate matter. This suggestion, to me at least, is an absurdity. In fairness, however, let us examine how it is proposed that the miracle of the living cell has evolved from inanimate molecules.

Which came first — nucleic acids or proteins?

All cells contain both nucleic acids and proteins, and cannot function without either. Thus proteins cannot be made without nucleic acids and nucleic acids need enzymes, that is protein, for their replication. This raises the fundamental difficulty that life, as we know it, depends on both nucleic acids and proteins, so that if each class of molecule needs each other, then which came first?

The German chemist, Manfred Eigen, has turned the Oparin-Haldane theory upside down and proposed that genes came first, suggesting the following scheme:

RNA $\longrightarrow$ genes $\longrightarrow$ enzymes $\longrightarrow$ cells

Eigen has argued that nucleic acid structure is relatively more simple than that of enzymes and that they are able to self-replicate, something proteins are unable to do. The double strands of DNA, for instance, separate on heating and recombine again on cooling. One suggestion is that replication originated in a situation where during daylight hours the temperature became such that primeval DNA strands separated and recombined when the temperature cooled at night.

If nucleic acids originated first, the immediate question is was it RNA or DNA? At the present time it is generally held that RNA came first because it has a much more diverse function than DNA. Furthermore, many biochemists argue that biosynthetic pathways in present-day organisms recapitulate what happened during chemical evolution. Accordingly, as ribose sugar is always formed first in today's metabolism and subsequently converted into deoxyribose, then RNA must have come before DNA.

The drawback to RNA being the first nucleic acid is that it is much more unstable that DNA. Thus when RNA is dissolved in water it readily breaks down into its components. It is therefore difficult to imagine how chemical evolution could have occurred with RNA as the sole primeval nucleic acid. This problem has been recognized by the Nobel prizewinner Francis Crick who has concluded: 'My own prejudice is that nucleic acid (probably RNA) came first closely followed by a simple form of protein synthesis. This seems to me the easiest route to follow, but even this appears fraught with difficulties.'[1]

Another Nobel prizewinner, Walter Gilbert, has also favoured a first form of life based on RNA. He envisaged an early life form consisting of self-replicating RNA molecules. Some of these molecules he proposes would have limited enzymic activity, hopefully just sufficient to carry out the replication process. This seems highly unlikely to me because for life to succeed replication has to be precisely controlled; although enzymes are able to do this in cells today, it is dubious whether RNA molecules could ever have performed the same task.

Speculation as to whether or not RNA could have been the first nucleic acid hinges on whether RNA could have formed spontaneously in the first place. There are two current suggestions for the origin of RNA. The first involves its formation in the deep mid-ocean ridge hydrothermal systems. This has it that RNA is formed within a zeolite matrix that not only retained the RNA molecules as they were formed, but also provided the catalytic activity needed for their synthesis. A second scenario is that the RNA molecules formed within pores of rock. Here there would have been a diversification of pore size, so there may have been sufficient selective pressure for the initial nucleic acids to begin making protein. These may have blocked pore channels and so favoured the synthesis of that particular type of RNA and so on. There is absolutely no experimental evidence for either of these suggestions. Therefore despite the many favourable aspects offered by these ideas, one must reach the inevitable conclusion that a primitive organism based on RNA does not seem likely principally because of the inherent chemical difficulties involved in producing an RNA molecule in the first place. Let us now consider some of these difficulties.

Firstly, it does not look plausible that the components of RNA could have appeared on the primitive earth in substantial amounts. The physicist Freeman Dyson has concluded: 'The result of 30 years of intensive chemical experimentation have shown that the pre-biotic synthesis of amino acids is easy to simulate but the pre-biotic synthesis of nucleotides is not.'[2]

Even if one were to assume that RNA components were present in the primeval soup, that is just the beginning of one's troubles. For how could they have joined together in the correct manner? Indeed this is more difficult to envisage for RNA than DNA. It all goes back to the number of joining steps necessary to form a RNA molecule. One immediately sees that the chances of making the right sort of RNA without ending up with large numbers of incorrectly made pieces is extremely remote. Furthermore, it is very difficult to think of a natural process that could select the correct one.

One is forced to admit that at present there is no theoretical model that could explain the spontaneous formation of nucleic acids, either RNA or DNA. Therefore the idea that nucleic acid was the first macromolecule on the primeval earth seems implausible. Did proteins therefore come first?

Freeman Dyson and other scientists have argued for a double-origin hypothesis. They claim that the very fact that life today is dependent upon both proteins and nucleic acids is a *prima facie* case for life beginning in two stages. Dyson argues: 'If we admit that the spontaneous emergence of protein structure and of nucleic acid out of molecular chaos are both unlikely, it is easier to imagine two unlikely events occurring separately over a long period of time than to imagine two unlikely events occurring simultaneously.'[3]

Freeman Dyson has likened the evolution of life to that of computers where the hardware is developed before the software. In this analogy the proteins are seen as the hardware and nucleic acids as the software. Although clearly it is rather a simplistic metaphor to use, he nevertheless continues by arguing that nucleic acids at some stage acted like a parasite and invaded the protein-based life to form ultimately a symbiotic interdependence — at which point the analogy to computers is irretrievably lost.

The first cell

Contained within the miraculous machinery of the living cell is an amazing mechanism of molecular regulation. Protein synthesis in particular is strictly controlled. The cell is programmed to manufacture a particular protein at precisely the moment it is required. Thus the cells of the eye lens during its formation make a series of proteins that result in a precise graduation of refractive index across the entire organ. An artificial plastic lens, for instance, has a uniform refractive index, and so is inferior to a natural one.[4]

Cell replication is also under rigid control. We all know what happens if cell replication goes out of control — it causes cancer. The precise mechanisms for control have eluded researchers completely.

Even in bacterial cells the expression of genes is carefully regulated. How could the extremely complex mechanisms for regulation have arisen? Could it have done so by blind chance?

In higher organisms cells differentiate into specialized cell types, each displaying specific characteristics. Again this is highly ordered and regulated. Could ordered behaviour have arisen from disorder? If chance did give rise to the first cell, would it not have been similar to a cancerous cell and merely divided *ad infinitum?* If so, evolution and progressive development would not have occurred. Yet even this type of cell seems too sophisticated to have arisen by blind chance.

In the light of the above remarks one is forced to adopt a somewhat jaundiced view of the experimental work that supposedly offers a mechanistic route to the origin of cells. This work begins with Oparin's coacervates.

In the 1930s Oparin attempted to reproduce some of the features of living cells using simple chemicals in the laboratory. His coacervates were droplets composed of a protein solution together with gum arabic. He showed that if an enzyme were to be incorporated into the droplet and its substrate dissolved in the surrounding solution, the droplet could be made to grow in size and eventually divide. This, Oparin declared, was analogous to cell division. The fallacy, of course, is that the initial enzyme had been isolated from a living cell. Furthermore, the materials from which he had constructed the coacervate droplet, namely, gum arabic and a natural protein, usually a histone, were both complicated natural biomolecules. And the solution contained only the substrate molecule and so little resembled the heterogeneous mixture that would have been present in the primeval soup. Oparin's coacervates therefore bear little relevance to the origins of the first cell.

Sidney Fox, of the University of Miami, has developed a second experimental scenario known as the proteinoid hypothesis. He believes that the first cells were droplets of polymerized amino acids or 'proteinoids'. Fox has argued from the fact that as amino acids are readily produced in primeval soup experiments, they would have become concentrated in pools on the primitive earth and in volcanic regions would have undergone polymerization. When the proteinoids so formed dissolved in water, they would have formed small microspheres bounded by a skin or 'membrane'. Fox further argued that these objects resembled cells and that they were capable of possessing a simple metabolism.

The proteinoid idea seems to be one up on that of Oparin's coacervates. Indeed, amino acids do polymerize if heated in the laboratory and there is no doubt there may have been many places on the primitive earth where similar reactions could have occurred. But could the primeval soup have produced pools of concentrated amino acids? It is more likely that the pools would have been mixtures of many thousands of substances, so any polymerization would have resulted in intractable tars and goos. Furthermore, because Fox's experiments produced microspheres, can these be likened to cells? Indeed is an apple an orange because it is round?

Those who argue that cells originated by some naturalistic mechanism such as that outlined above may differ in favouring a particular route, but they are generally agreed on the fact that the first cells must have been heterotrophs, that is, they would have derived nourishment from outside sources. These cells would have lacked an intrinsic metabolism and depended entirely on the constituents of the primeval soup for their diet. As the food supply ran out they would themselves have devised ways for the manufacture of substances they required; in other words, they would have developed a metabolism. Is such a scenario possible? The principal problem is how in the first place they could have recognized particular molecules. It is difficult to see how they could have discriminated between glycine and alanine, let alone between the optical isomers of alanine. Thus before a complicated metabolism could have developed it would have been necessary to have a means of distinguishing one molecule from another. Until this was achieved it is very difficult to see how the sophisticated chemistry needed to make proteins and enzymes could have developed.

Prokaryotes and eukaryotes

Since the advent of the electron microscope in the early 1950s a new classification of cells has been developed. All organisms have been classed as either prokaryotes (from Greek *pro*, meaning before, and *karyon*, kernel) or, *eukaryote* (from Greek *eu*, meaning true).

Prokaryotes, which include all bacteria and various other micro-organisms, have no distinct nucleus; whereas eukaryotes (all other cell types) have the DNA assembled into chromosomes and packaged within a membrane into the cell's nucleus.

The realization of this fact makes any mechanistic explanation for the origin of cells even more dubious. Not only is it necessary to find a mechanism for how molecules may have organized themselves to form the simplest cells, the prokaryotes, but one must now explain how and, more intriguingly why, they became eukaryotes.

If cells arose on the primeval earth by blind chance, why didn't prokaryotes remain as prokaryotes? What was the advantage in becoming a eukaryote? In other words, why didn't the earth simply remain populated with micro-organisms? Professor W. S. Bullough of Birkbeck College has referred to the transition of prokaryotes into eukaryotes as 'one of the greatest single advances in the whole course of evolution'. Yet no one can explain how it happened, or indeed why.

The popular theory, at the moment, has been developed by Lynn Margulis and is explained in her book *Origin of Eukaryotic Cells*, published in 1970. She argues that eukaryotic cells have evolved as a consequence of parasitism and symbiosis. She believes that the big steps in cellular evolution occurred because of parasites. Thus the principal organelles in higher cells are descended from independent living organisms which had previously invaded them. Eventually the invading organism and its host would have developed some form of mutual dependence.

The interior of eukaryotic cells does indeed contain many specialized particles known as 'organelles'. Each type of organelle has a different task to perform and so the workings of the cell

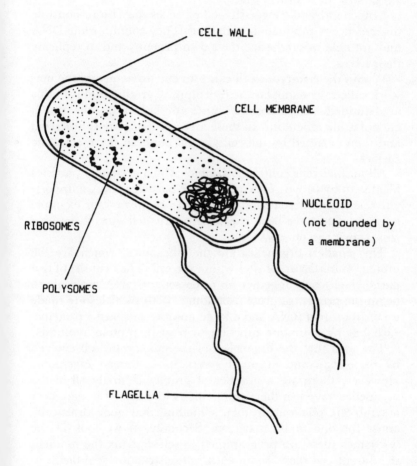

FIGURE 7

Structural features of a typical prokaryotic cell

are isolated into different regions. The nucleus itself is separated from the rest of the cell by a nuclear envelope, within which the DNA is coiled up into a dense mass known as chromatin. At the heart of the nucleus is the nucleolus in which the ribosomes are constructed.

Mitochondria are cigar-shaped particles that are responsible for the energy production of the cell. They contain some DNA and are able to synthesize their own proteins and to replicate themselves.

Within the eukaryotic cell exists an extensive membrane network called the endoplasmic reticulum. Certain regions of this are studded with ribosomes and are known as the rough endoplasmic reticulum. In these areas proteins are synthesized and then excreted by the cell via the pores in the membrane surface.

All animal cells contain lysosomes which are small particles filled with hydrolytic enzymes. These particles play an important role in the destruction of foreign organisms, for example bacteria, that have been captured by the cell during the process known as phagocytosis.

The smallest organelles are the ribosomes, which are the protein-manufacturing sites within the cell. They consist of two parts which come together on a messenger RNA molecule to begin the process of protein-building. Both particles are made up of ribosomal RNA and a large number of specific proteins, each having a unique function to play in protein synthesis.

The idea that the organelles of the eukaryotic cell evolved by parasitism and eventual symbiosis is indeed ingenious. However, there are a number of problems: firstly all of the organelles have lost their autonomous identity. If it were ever a symbiotic relationship then something has gone drastically amiss for one of the partners. Secondly, if we look at the lysosomes these are programmed to self-destruct the moment the parent cell dies. Again such self-destruction is difficult to account for if it had originated in a symbiotic partnership. Finally, where does one draw the line: did the nucleus itself originate by parasitism? And what about the ribosomes?

In eukaryotic plants the chloroplast is believed to have developed from a cyanobacterium (i.e. blue-green alga). The drawback to this is that blue-green alga lack chlorophyll b and

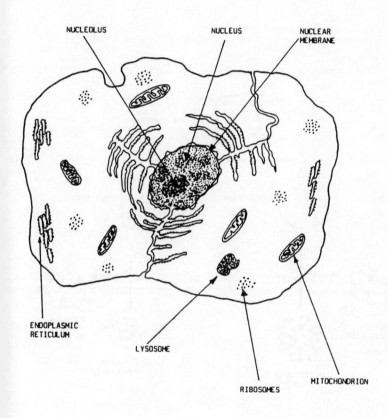

FIGURE 8

Structural components of a typical eukaryotic cell.

have a photosynthetic system based on light-sensitive materials known as phycobilin-proteins. This is a further argument against the idea that eukaryotic cells originated by a series of symbiotic adaptations.

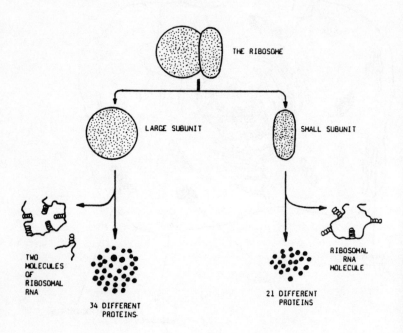

FIGURE 9

The ribosome is the protein factory of the cell. The illustration shows that even the ribosome of a bacterium is highly complex and consists of both RNA molecules and a large number of specific protein molecules.

Origin of photosynthesis

The origin of photosynthesis has key significance in the story of life on the earth. Thus when photosynthesis first occurred it resulted in the release of free oxygen into the atmosphere. The fundamental reaction in photosynthesis is very simple, being:

$$\text{carbon dioxide} + \text{water} \xrightarrow{\text{light}} \text{sugar} + \text{oxygen}.$$

It is argued that the birth of photosynthesis in green plants had momentous consequences, for oxygen would have been released into the atmosphere for the first time and organisms, such as ourselves, depending on aerobic respiration, could have developed. But could the process of photosynthesis have evolved?

The precise details of photosynthesis might serve to confuse the general reader, therefore let us take a superficial look at what occurs when light falls upon a plant leaf.

Firstly, the apparatus for collecting that sunlight is located within the membranes of the chloroplasts. Specific pigments are responsible for the efficient capture of the light, the major one being chlorophyll a. This pigment is closely associated with a number of specific proteins also located within the chloroplast membrane. Also associated with the chlorophyll are certain other accessory pigments that include carotenoids and the phycobilins. These may be likened to an array of optical telescopes in which light is collected and passed on to a central computer for processing.

All the molecules involved in photosynthesis are extremely complicated. Not only are there pigment molecules involved, but also specific proteins. Could such a complex arrangement have arisen by blind chance? Any reasonable scientist is forced to express his doubts about this.

Origin of viruses

Finally, we come to the vexed problem concerning the origin of viruses. Until quite recently this subject was rarely discussed, even among scientists. Indeed, it was very difficult to find anything written on the subject even in textbooks on virology. Then along came AIDS and everything changed. Now we find frequent speculation on the origin of viruses in the morning newspapers and it has become a subject of agitated debate.

The discontinuity between living organisms and the inanimate world has always intrigued philosophers. If inanimate matter were to be transformed into living organisms then one would expect there to be some transitional forms. This was the hope, at least in the early 1950s, before the science of molecular biology got under way. Today, however, this hope has been shattered. Instead of discovering a transitional form of life from which the first cell may have evolved, all molecular biology has done is to illuminate the vast void that exists between life and non-life.

At one time it was hoped that certain viruses might prove to be intermediate between the physical and biological world. It seemed attractive to treat viruses as primitive micro-organisms that had not reached the full status of being alive. J. B. S. Haldane was one of the first to consider viruses as a form of 'half-life'.

This view is considered today to be wrong. All viruses appear to be totally parasitic and so must have originated after cells had developed. The most general view is that they are derived from plasmids, i.e. fragments of DNA that have detached themselves from the cell's DNA, and by some mysterious mechanism they have found a way of coating themselves with a protein shell so enabling themselves to survive alone outside the cell.

If this is so, one is left with the problem of how the original piece of DNA managed to get out of the cell, and how it acquired a protein shell? Much more difficult to answer is the fundamental problem of where the virus acquired the genes needed to make just those specific enzymes necessary for it to infect its host cell and to multiply successfully when once inside. To these questions there is no ready answer. One is therefore left wondering whether the present explanation of viral origin within the framework of evolution is a total misconception.

8. Panspermia

One solution to the problem of the origin of life on earth is to propose that it arrived here from somewhere else in the universe. In recent years science fiction writers have been joined by Academician Oparin in suggesting that, at some time in the past, celestial astronauts landed on the virgin earth and after finding it to be uninteresting, departed leaving behind some waste debris from which our own life developed. An extension of this moonshine is that proposed by the Tokyo biochemist Tairo Oshima, who believed the nucleotide sequence in the DNA of a bacteriophage to be a cosmic message from a superior intelligence located somewhere else in the cosmos.

The concept of 'panspermia', which means, 'The germs of life are all over the universe,' is derived from the work of the German chemist Justus von Liebig. He believed that there were vast areas of interstellar space occupied by the 'germs of life'. This idea was further developed by the Swedish physical chemist Svante Arrhenius, who proposed in his book *World in the Making* (1908) that spores of living matter could be passed from one celestial body to another. He argued that they were propelled by light rays and he went on to calculate that a spore travelling from the earth through space would reach the outer realms of the solar system in about fourteen months and in 9000 years arrive at our nearest star, Alpha Centauri.

An earlier version of this idea was put forward by the German biologist H. E. Richter, who proposed that it was the rapid motion of celestial bodies that detached spores into space. Richter gave the name 'cosmozoa' to his space-travelling spores.

One cannot deny that even today the surface of the earth

is bombarded with extraterrestrial material. Rough estimates indicate that around 1000 tons of such material reach the earth's surface every day. By measuring the distribution of the element nickel in sections of Antarctic ice it has been possible to check the rate of extraterrestrial deposition over past history. These measurements indicate that there has been little change. Extraterrestrial material is one thing, but panspermia is something completely different. There is absolutely no evidence to suggest that any of the material arriving on the earth from outer space has any capacity for life. Apart from this lack of direct evidence there are other serious objections to the theory of panspermia.

Firstly, it is difficult to envisage how any living material, dormant or otherwise, could survive the exposure to ionizing and ultraviolet radiation that it would inevitably encounter during the long period of transit from one planetary system to another.

Secondly, Arrhenius maintained that the spores of panspermia were propelled through space by the radiation pressure of the parent star — a sort of solar wind. If this were so, then the same sort of energy would repel the spore as it approached a new star and so it would never land on any planet.

Thirdly, there is no evidence that the earth is sending out any 'panspermia' into the depths of space.

Finally, for panspermia to be credible a planet must send an immense amount of material out into space, if there is to be any chance of its reaching another possible life-bearing planet. In fact, some calculations indicate that *so much* would have to leave any one planet as to make the whole idea unreasonable.

Directed panspermia

Although the concept of panspermia has generally received a cold shoulder by the majority of scientists, it has nevertheless been revamped by Francis Crick and Leslie Orgel. Their version is called 'directed panspermia'.

Crick is a theoretical biologist of enormous stature within the scientific community, so any theory with which he is associated cannot readily be dismissed. One might well ask, 'Why has he ventured to speculate in this field?' One finds from his writings over the years that he has become progressively disillusioned with the plausibility of the primeval soup concept. As discussed in chapter 3, the primeval soup theory depends upon having a primitive earth with a reducing atmosphere. This is now thought of as highly unlikely. Furthermore Crick, more than anyone, appreciates the important implications of molecular biology, namely that it is inconceivable that even the simplest cell could have originated by chance. In his book *Life Itself* he writes, 'An honest man, armed with all the knowledge available to us now, could only state that in some sense, the origin of life appears at the moment to be almost a miracle, so many are the conditions which would have had to have been satisfied to get it going.'[1]

To Crick, the avowed atheist, if the primeval soup is now redundant, then there is no alternative other than some sort of panspermia. To use his own words, 'Orgel and I hit upon the idea of Directed Panspermia' and 'we published it quietly in *Icarus*' (*Icarus* is a popular science journal).[2] I must add at this juncture that I find his claim to have 'hit upon' the theory rather difficult to swallow. Directed panspermia is simply not an original theory, for J. B. S. Haldane had suggested in 1954 that the earth was seeded with what he called 'astroplankton' by extraterrestrial intelligent beings. Crick's version is almost identical to that of Haldane.

There is a curious phenomenon in science known as the 'phantom hypothesis'. To illustrate my meaning let us suppose some individual publishes a completely new theory which is so revolutionary that it is immediately treated with ridicule and scorn and its originator is branded a bonehead and a charlatan. The idea is dismissed out of hand. This becomes a phantom hypothesis when someone of importance in the scientific community picks it up and repackages it. Instead of derision it now meets with acceptance simply because of the particular person's prestige. A good example is that of Charles Darwin and his *Origin of Species*. Several years before Darwin published his theory Chambers had published exactly the same idea in his book the *Vestiges of Creation*. Chambers's theory was treated with universal ridicule, yet when Darwin put forward the same idea a few years later it met with universal acclaim.

We have the same phenomenon with Crick. His idea of

directed panspermia is nothing more nor less than a clever repackaging of van Daniken's theory related in his notorious book *The Chariots of the Gods*. But whereas van Daniken is ignored and has largely become a figure of fun in the scientific community, Crick's theory has been treated with serious reverence.

Let us look at the details of Crick's phantom theory. Firstly, directed panspermia makes the basic assumption that there is life elsewhere in the universe. It proclaims that like a hive of bees in summer, a life-bearing planet would during a particular period in its life-cycle swarm by the random dispersal of colonizing packages into the void of the universe.

The most likely vector for directed panspermia would have been micro-organisms, as these would be able to survive the long journey through space, as well as requiring little maintenance. Crick speculates that these microbes would have been encapsulated into the nose cone of a spacecraft. On reaching the earth this vessel would have plunged into the oceans that by then were a virgin soup of organic matter.

So this is how life was seeded on the earth. One is left wondering how the spacecraft's door opened after a journey of several million years. American and Soviet space probes today don't seem to have the capacity to operate after only a few years! What technology would be required to develop machinery that remained in good working order after a couple of million years? Furthermore, if the spacecraft had landed in the mud at the bottom of the ocean might it not have become fossilized? If one craft reached the earth, why not others? Why don't we find them today, either newly arrived or fossilized?

The case for directed panspermia

Let us examine in detail the argument for directed panspermia. Firstly, there is the anomaly that within all living organisms the element molybdenum is more abundant than one would expect from its natural distribution within the earth's surface. Crick argues that this is suggestive that life arose not on the earth but on a planet that had a surface crust much richer in this element.

Secondly, there is the anomaly of the earliest fossilized organisms in earth rocks. These appear to resemble blue-green algae. Yet these rocks date from a relatively early time in the life of the earth, so early in fact that it is a considerable embarrassment to evolutionists who know that life could not have evolved to that level of sophistication in the short time available. Either the dating procedures are wrong, or those algae did not originate on earth.

Thirdly, there is the fact that the genetic code appears to be uniform throughout the natural world. There is no remnant of a precursor code, which suggests that the genetic code did not evolve on earth but came fully developed in the first organism to reach earth from somewhere in the depths of space.

Finally, and along the same lines, there is the remarkable fact that all life appears to be constructed of the same basic building blocks. That is, the biochemistry of life on earth is surprisingly uniform. This seems to suggest that life must have originated at one definite point in time. The idea of random chance being responsible in a primeval soup scenario seems most implausible. This observation neatly fits in with the view that all the pathways of metabolism could have been worked out elsewhere.

Problems with directed panspermia

Let us look in turn at the anomalies on which Crick bases his theory. Firstly, the fact that the element molybdenum is more abundant in organisms today than one might expect is not necessarily proof that life came from another planet, which had a greater abundance of this element. This argument is based on what one might expect to find and I think most scientists would concede that in research the unexpected is frequently encountered. When this is the case it nearly always follows as a consequence of our lack of understanding in a particular field. There could be many other reasons why molybdenum is present to the extent that it is within organisms. It is rather naïve to adopt the simplistic view that it must be related to the composition of the environment.

Secondly, the discovery of the blue-green algae in the earliest rocks need not indicate that they were the very earliest organisms. It is very difficult to conceive of any more primitive organism being preserved in the fossil record. It is highly speculative therefore to suppose that the blue-green algae fossils, because they are the earliest to be preserved, must therefore have been the first form of earth life.

The most obvious fallacy of the panspermia saga is that it solves nothing. It simply shifts the problem of the origin of life to another corner of the universe. This aspect will be discussed in more detail in a subsequent chapter.

Besides this there are a number of other flaws. Firstly, although it is questionable whether we can reliably estimate the age of the universe, the value most acceptable today leaves little time for life to have originated by chance and developed elsewhere to such an extent as to be able to send life-bearing spores to the earth at least three billion years ago. There simply does not appear to have been enough time for this to have transpired.

One might well add that all this is unlikely on another count. Let us suppose that the peoples of the planet shedding spores had reached a technology much like what we have today. If they despatched the original spores three to four billion years ago, then what happened to that civilization? Look at ourselves. In little more than a century we have progressed from John Dalton's simple atomic theory to a miraculous vision of the gene now provided by the science of molecular biology; we have gone from the penny-farthing to the Space Shuttle. If this progress is possible in a hundred years, what is possible in a thousand, indeed a million years? We are now envisaging a civilization three billion years on. Why didn't life on that planet develop even further, so that some more sophisticated package could have been sent towards earth? Why did they just send micro-organisms? Surely in the vastness of the time available that civilization should have been able to improve upon the initial package. Maybe an improved package would have overtaken the earlier ones. But there is no evidence that this is so. To suppose that the civilization was on the verge of extinction and so motivated to send out spores is to opt out.

This leads naturally to a fundamental puzzle: why would they have wanted to send spores in the first place? Presumably it was to enable life to form elsewhere, that is, to replicate intelligent life as it had formed on that planet. This is where a fatal flaw occurs in the whole concept. Evolution, so it is argued, occurs entirely by chance; its purpose, or end product, is not intelligent life. The dinosaurs are said to have lasted 140 million years and would have survived longer if a chance event had not led to their extinction. There is no overall blue-print in evolution. If the human race becomes extinct following a nuclear war the insects will take over — evolution is completely meaningless. If life had been sent here by spores of panspermia from an intelligent civilization, they would not have relied upon pure chance to ensure other intelligent creatures to evolve. They would have built into the first organisms determinants that would have ensured that intelligent life arose much more quickly than it apparently has done on earth. Furthermore, they would not have left it to chance. This is not beyond what might be possible with the present techniques of genetic engineering. It would have been easily accomplished by a civilization having the technology to send viable spores in a space vehicle on a journey of several million years! But they didn't do this; evolution as it is seen today is meaningless and progresses not according to an overall plan, but by random chance. *If this is so then life could not have originated from a higher civilization in some distant part of the cosmos.*

9. Life from meteorites?

As we have seen in the previous chapter, the concept of directed panspermia belongs to the realm of science fiction — and rightly so. However, it has been argued for many years that life may have originated on the earth by 'seeds' arriving from another corner of the cosmos, not by design but by accident. It is a loop-hole that has been snapped up by many scientists as a way of escape from the inevitable conclusion that life simply could not have originated on the earth via the primeval soup mechanism. These scientists argue that as there are many planets and comets in the universe that are much older than the earth, then on a purely statistical basis it is much more likely that life originated on them.

One of the first proponents of this idea in modern times was the German mineralogist Hieronymus Richter. He argued that as many meteors encounter the earth's atmosphere at an oblique angle they are immediately ejected back into space after penetrating only a little distance. Nevertheless during this brief encounter with the earth they may pick up innumerable living cells and spores that have been carried up from the earth's surface into the atmosphere on rising air currents. Richter argued that it was in this way that a meteorite many years ago may have transferred life from some other planet to our own.

Meteorites and the earth

Every day about 1000 tons of cosmic dust reach the earth's surface from outer space. One tenth of this mass is in the form of meteorites. It is quite likely that during the early history of the earth this meteorite deposition was in fact considerably greater than it is today.

The earliest recorded incidence of a meteorite shower is contained in the Bible. In the book of Joshua we read, 'And it came to pass, as they fled from before Israel, and were in the going down to Beth-horon, that the Lord cast down great stones from heaven upon them unto Azekah, and they died' (Joshua 10:11).

Meteors start heating up about seventy-five miles above the earth's surface; consequently small meteors burn up as they traverse the atmosphere and experience friction against air molecules. They become heated to incandescence and we see them as 'shooting stars'. Most ultimately disintegrate. Some, having a mass greater than 10 kilograms, may survive to reach the earth's surface. During descent their surfaces heat up, yet the bulk of the interior remains relatively unaffected. Large meteors are sometimes referred to as fireballs; these usually break up in mid-air creating a shower of smaller ones. It is possible that it was one of these we find described in the book of Joshua.

It is estimated that around 2000 meteorites fall on the earth every year, but as many of them fall into the oceans only a few are actually recovered. The ones that are may be classified into three main types:

1. stone meteorites;
2. iron meteorites
3. a mixture of 1 and 2.

About 90% of all meteorites may be classified as stone meteorites. Of these 3% are known as carbonaceous chondrites. These have proved to be the most interesting and have been divided into three types (I, II and III), depending upon their carbon content. Type I carbonaceous chondrites have a fine grain structure and contain about 3.5% carbon. Type II are termed 'chondrules' and contain about 2.5% carbon, but also sulphur. Type III have the lowest amount of carbon of around 0.5%.

Large meteorites strike the earth with such tremendous force that they become deeply buried beneath the surface. The heat produced may cause some of its outer surface to vaporize and the gases produced may immediately create an explosion, completely shattering the meteorite and forming a huge crater on the surface. There are many large craters that exist which bear witness to such impacts. One of the largest is the huge Meteor Crater near Winslow in Arizona. Only a small number of large meteorites have been discovered intact. One weighing about sixty tons was found near Grootfontein in South Africa, and another one in Greenland weighed thirty-seven tons.

The search for life in meteorites

The history of the search for life in meteorites is one of intrigue, rivalry and insanity. Let us begin at the beginning. It was not until the nineteenth century that it became accepted that meteorites originated from outer space. Previous to this there was bitter controversy concerning their origin.

One account that has come down to us concerns the astronomer Sir William Herschel. It is told that during a drinking session in an Oxford tavern some time in the early 1760s he, in jest, put forward the suggestion that not only did meteorites come from outer space but that they also brought with them new forms of life. This was not meant to be taken seriously, but to his surprise eager students took up the idea and spread it about. It was only in later years that Herschel came to see that the idea did in fact have some virtue.

The idea was not completely forgotten for in 1834 J. J. Berzelius published the first analysis of organic compounds in the Alais meteorite. Berzelius and his student Wöhler detected a number of hydrocarbons in the meteorite and concluded that there was a possibility that they might have had a biological origin. He concluded that the analysis may have been 'a hint concerning the presence of organic structures in other planetary bodies.' [1]

In 1864 the prodigious Pasteur took up the problem and unsuccessfully tried to detect micro-organisms in the Orgueil meteorite. At this stage the story begins to take a rather bizarre twist. It begins with the claim, made in 1879 by Otto Hahn, in a book entitled *Die Urzelle,* that meteorites contain fossilized marine plants and animals. By making photographic thin sections of the Knyahinya meteorite, Hahn believed he had discovered traces of previously live organisms. More discoveries followed and were published in his 1880 volume *Die Meteorite* and *Ihre Organismen*. An immediate scientific controversy blew up. The French Academy claimed it was a scientific error of the greatest magnitude. And in the United States, Professor Hawes of the Smithsonian Institute resorted to direct character assassination, claiming that 'Dr Hahn is a kind of half-insane man, whose imagination has run away with him.'[2]

Nevertheless Hahn's work received wide circulation in the popular press and was taken up enthusiastically in his own country by D. F. Weinland, an established palaeontologist. Weinland went further and claimed to have confirmed Hahn's theory by actually identifying the marine organisms in meteorites and concluded that all meteorites 'give the impression of a common creation, which without doubt affected a single extraterrestrial celestial body'.[3]

The end came in 1882 when C. Vogt, a Swiss geologist, then President of the National Institute of Geneva, published a study on several meteorites concluding that there were no fossils in meteorites and that all those identified by Hahn and Weinland were simply artefacts.

This was the last straw for Hahn who threw in the towel and gave up all future micropalaeontological work. He subsequently emigrated to Canada in disgrace and today his famous collection of over 800 meteorite sections rests in the Royal Ontario Museum in Toronto.

Following this episode the question whether meteorites contained life forms was largely forgotten for almost half a century. Then followed what was probably the most bizarre incident of all. It began in 1921 when two French scientists, Galippe and Souffland, published in the proceedings of the Academy of Sciences in Paris the extraordinary claim that on heating mineralized organisms to a high temperature the actual process of mineralization could be reversed. The fossilized organism could be brought back to life. These scientists went on further to claim that they had been able to 'revive' more than twenty different fossilized organisms from the Meunier meteorite. This was achieved by heating them to 335°C. Furthermore they supported these findings by claiming that Professor Lacroix, the

Director of the famous Mont-Pélé Institute, had achieved similar remarkable transformations before his death.

The claim that life could be created from inanimate matter is a frequent story-line in early twentieth-century fiction. One is left intrigued as to why the Academy of Sciences in Paris published Galippe and Souffland's work, which seems to us today so utterly preposterous. If it was all a deliberate hoax, why?

Bacteria in meteorites

In contrast to the French claims to have revitalized fossilized bacteria from meteorites, American scientists went one better, when in 1932 Dr C. B. Lipman claimed to have isolated viable bacteria in the interior of nine different meteorites. He wrote, 'Stony meteorites bring down with them from somewhere in space a few surviving bacteria, probably in spore form . . . which can be made to grow on bacteriological media in the laboratory.'[4]

Lipman, who was Dean of the University of California, had earlier made claims that he could detect viable micro-organisms in ancient rocks such as coal. Lipman, who always performed his work taking the most rigid precautions to prevent contamination, postulated that the microbes he had detected had become embedded in the rocks during their formation.

Lipman's meteorite findings were highly controversial and attracted much interest. However, most scientists who repeated his work reached the conclusion that Lipman's discoveries were almost certainly due to contamination. One researcher, H.N. Nininger, concluded that the 'supposition of the presence of living bacteria in meteorites is nonsense'.[5]

However, the concurrent studies on the microbiology of ancient rocks did seem to suggest that micro-organisms might be preserved during rock formation. Thus A. Rippel in 1935 found that after dissolution of Permian salt crystals he could find the remains of dead bacteria. These findings have been recently confirmed by H. Dombrowski who in 1963 isolated seven different strains of bacteria in a single salt crystal. Furthermore, he went on to demonstrate that it was possible to embed present-day bacteria into salt crystals without them losing their viability. Even after storage within the salt crystal for a whole year, the organisms remained viable.

These findings revived the controversy regarding whether micro-organisms could occur in meteorites. In 1961 Dr F. Sisler, at the American Assocation for the Advancement of Science meeting, reported that he had succeeded in culturing micro-organisms from the Murray meteorite. Because they exhibited sluggish growth, unusual morphology and a lack of pathogenicity, he concluded that they must be of extraterrestrial origin. However, Sisler's work was received with so much scepticism that he abandoned it entirely.

Proof that all the work so far described was due to contamination came from the Russian scientist A. A. Imshenetsky. In his book *Life Sciences and Space Research* published in 1964, he reported that solid rocks such as basalt, if buried in soil, could easily become contaminated by micro-organisms even in their central regions. On this basis he concluded that all previous reports of bacteria in meteorites were due to contamination.

Imshenetsky went further and claimed that even the micro-fossils in some carbonaceous chondrites were almost certainly artefacts having been carried into the interior by water seepage.

A detailed confirmation of these findings was published in the New York Academy of Sciences in 1972. In this work G. Claus and P. P. Madri studied 432 meteorite samples and in none of them, either on the surface or the interior, could they discover any sign of micro-organisms.

Regardless of these seemingly conclusive scientific findings the subject still seems capable of stirring up bitter controversy. As recently as November 1981 there took place a most acrimonious debate on the subject following a public lecture in Cardiff. And N. W. Pirie at a Royal Society meeting in 1981 completely opened up the debate anew by claiming that 'Microscopic structures in some meteorites resemble biological structures closely and they are too abundant and uniformly distributed throughout the stone to be contaminants.'[6]

One may conclude that the scientific evidence for the presence of bacteria in meteorites cannot stand critical examination. Nevertheless some scientists continue to cling desperately to their castle in the air.

Biochemicals in meteorites?

The failure to prove the presence of micro-organisms in meteorites has spurred researchers to look for other signs of life, such as the presence of known biochemicals. This is again another story of discovery, refutation and controversy.

The problem with this type of study is that the meteorites must be obtained as soon as possible after they arrive on earth. They must be as free as possible from contamination with terrestrial products. And the biochemicals must be isolated, preferably from the interior, and then be identified.

Contamination is always a problem in this type of research as many meteorites have complex networks of deep cracks that extend to their interior. Carbonaceous chondrites, in particular, are extremely porous and friable so that they may readily absorb terrestrial contaminants — even more so if they have undergone eager handling by collectors.

Between 2-6% of the insoluble organic matter of meteorites has been found by Drs J. Brooks and G. Shaw of Bradford University to resemble sporopollenin. Sporopollenin is the very stable material of which pollen capsules are made. It is this substance that enables pollen to survive in ancient sediments. (The significance of this finding will be discussed in detail shortly.)

On 28 September 1969 the famous Murchison meteorite fell in Australia. The first studies on it were published by K. Kvenvolden and his collaborators in the journal *Nature* some time in 1970. [7] They reported finding racemic (i.e. D,L) amino acids in the interior region of it. They then concluded that as amino acids occur in living organisms as the L-isomer, then the amino acids in the Murchison meteorite could not have arisen by terrestrial contamination. Furthermore many of the amino acids were unusual and not the sort found in the proteins of terrestrial organisms, for example α-amino butyric acid and pipecolic acid. Kvenvolden concluded therefore that he had discovered amino acids of extraterrestrial origin. On 2 December 1970 NASA announced to the world: 'The first positive identification of amino acids of extraterrestrial origin has been made . . . The find is probably the first conclusive proof of extraterrestrial chemical evolution.' [8]

Yet, over a decade later, this meteorite still continues to cause controversy. Engel and Nagy have reported during 1982 in *Nature* that several of the amino acids are, in fact, only partially racemized. They concluded that the original amino acids in the meteorite were completely racemic but that during its descent to earth some of the amino acids may have undergone some sort of stereoselective decomposition. [9]

Conclusion

At best one cannot be absolutely certain that, whatever one finds in a meteorite, it did not originate on the earth itself. Even if the meteorite were to have been collected soon after landing and if it had the minimum of handling, one can never be sure that it hadn't picked up biological material from a previous encounter with the earth. It is now known that some meteorites collide with the earth's atmosphere and are immediately ejected back into space, only to return many years later.

However, common sense tells us that there is not life outside the earth. Any biological molecules found on meteorites must have originated, one way or another, on earth. The fact that the Apollo lunar samples failed to indicate biochemicals confirms the view that life is only present here on earth. If meteorites were loaded with biochemicals then one would have expected to find a thick layer of organic dust on the surface of the moon. This was not so.

I believe there is a simple explanation for the presence of biochemicals in meteorites. They arise from contamination by pollen grains. Immense quantities of pollen are driven up into the upper atmosphere by air currents. During the descent of any meteorite the pollen grains become embedded into its surface cracks. Within the pollen shell are an abundance of amino acids. They are all of the L-type, but as the meteorite becomes hot, the amino acids racemize. Finally, as it passes through layers of cloud, water droplets wash out the amino acids from the pollen grains to leave a shell of sporopollenin. What Brooks and Shaw had found was indeed sporopollenin.

Proof of this suggestion comes from an inspection of the types

of amino acid found in meteorites. They resemble very much
the amino acids present in honey; take for example, pipecolic
acid, α-amino butyric acid and β-alanine. These amino acids
arise in honey from pollen. In fact the amino acids found in
meteorites are characteristic of pollen. Pipecolic acid, for
instance, is characteristic of grass pollen.

The presence of biochemicals in meteorites does not indicate,
as many would like to think, the possibility of extraterrestrial
life, nor indeed extraterrestrial chemical evolution. They arise
from pollen grains that are picked up by the meteorite as it
falls to earth.

10. Life from space?

Another eminent scientist who has become discontented with the primeval soup hypothesis, and probably the most vocal, has been Sir Fred Hoyle. Born in Bingley, Yorkshire, in 1915, the son of a wool merchant, he has been likened to that other polemic Yorkshireman Mr Geoffrey Boycott. Hoyle has always been ready to question the orthodox and arouse controversy. Much of this has been skilfully dramatized. Thus he is probably the only scientist to have appealed to the Prime Minister over the rejection of a research proposal. And how many other visiting lecturers to the Royal Institution have had the protection of Special Branch detectives? He has not only proved a thorn in the flesh to the world of science, but has also sent reverberations through the sedate world of archaeology by his support for the theory that Stonehenge was an astrological computer. And to cap it all he has recently caused commotion among the dinosaurs at the British Museum by his claim that the crucial 'missing-link' fossil, *Archaeopteryx*, is a fake.

Since he resigned his Cambridge chair amid rumours of plots against him by intensely jealous colleagues, he has published with his collaborator, Chandra Wickramasinghe, a string of books all challenging the basic tenets of conventional biology. That these challenges to biology should come from an astronomer cum science fiction writer, and a professor of Applied Mathematics, is surprising. One may point out, however, that the hub of their work is related to the mathematics of probability. Both Hoyle and Wickramasinghe argue that the chance for life to have arisen spontaneously from the primeval soup is so remote as to be impossible. They use a now famous metaphor, comparing the chance formation of life to that of a tornado sweeping through a junk-yard and assembling a Boeing 747 from the materials found there. [1]

They take this even further and argue that the whole of conventional cosmological thinking must be in error because present ideas concerning the age of the cosmos would not have allowed sufficient time for the chance development of life on earth.

These represent two challenges to present orthodoxy that no one should ignore. As we shall see later, there is much to ridicule in Hoyle's writings, but these two central attacks on the primeval soup scenario cannot be dismissed lightly. Hoyle himself has commented: 'We did not arrive at our ideas at all light-heartedly.' [2]

Apart from the probability factor, Hoyle attacks the soup theory on three main issues:

(i) From recent geochemical evidence it appears unlikely that the earth had a reducing atmosphere.

(ii) It is difficult to understand why so few biochemicals are employed by living cells today. If life arose in a soup containing an infinite variety of chemicals, then one would have expected many more to be employed in the workings of living cells today.

(iii) That the Miller-type experiments do not, in fact, mimic the real conditions that existed on the primeval earth.

Hoyle has gone on to conclude that 'In accepting the primeval soup theory of the origin of life scientists have replaced the religious mysteries which shrouded this question with equally mysterious scientific dogmas.' [3]

However, Hoyle's ideas are a little confusing. For instance, he strongly denies that life could arise spontaneously from the primeval soup on earth, but believes it occurred in a primeval soup somewhere in space. What is the difference? His argument has been that there is only one earth but billions of comets in outer space. But one could argue that although there is but one earth, there could nevertheless be billions of little ponds of primeval soup across the surface of it. What is the difference? Hoyle simply shifts the problem from the earth to a position in outer space. This solves nothing; in fact it creates new problems.

Let us look in detail at the development of Hoyle's ideas. This is probably best done by following the chronological order of their development in his published books. We find his thinking to have developed along the following lines:

1. First we find him completely disillusioned with the primeval soup scenario. This problem is the impetus for all his subsequent work.

2. He maintains that the origin of the earth's atmosphere and oceans is from a collision with an ice-comet at some point in the earth's early history.

3. A further comet collided with the earth about four billion years ago bringing with it the 'seeds' of life.

4. That even today micro-organisms continually fall on the earth from outer space. These microbes cause world epidemics.

5. This idea is developed further in that not only do micro-organisms fall on the earth from outer space, but also naked genes. These specific genes may become incorporated into the genetic material of earthly organisms causing mutations and so evolution.

I think this is a fair synopsis of his ideas. Let us now look at them in detail. Firstly, in *Lifecloud* (1978) Hoyle puts forward his argument that life could not have arisen spontaneously in a primeval soup. He then proposes that chemical evolution is much more likely to have occurred on particles of graphite within the immense dust clouds of interstellar space.

Evidence for this is the infra-red spectra of the dust clouds obtained from satellite measurements. This work confirms that many simple organic substances are present in interstellar space, including formaldehyde ($HCHO$), methanol ($CH_3 OH$), formamide ($HCONH_2$), methylamine (CH_3NH_2), acetaldehyde (CH_3CHO) and ethanol (CH_3CH_2OH).

The most ubiquitous substance appears to be formaldehyde ($HCHO$). Hoyle argues that compression of gas clouds containing formaldehyde would generate polysaccharides, which do indeed have the same empirical formula. In particular the most abundant polysaccharide on earth, cellulose, would have been formed on a large scale in outer space.

Hoyle supports this argument by quoting the abundant evidence for organic molecules in space, from studies on carbonaceous meteorites. In a further book, *Space Travellers* (1981), he writes, 'The facts of astronomy point strongly to interstellar space being chock-a-block with biological material.'[4]

The main argument against these ideas may be summarized as follows.

Firstly, interstellar gas clouds would be too thin to allow chemical evolution. In other words, it seems more preposterous to suggest that life originated in interstellar space than to accept the primeval soup scenario.

Secondly, the finding of cellulose in interstellar gas clouds is possible — but so what? Cellulose is very similar to the inert polymer polythene. The discovery of cellulose, even if it were confirmed, proves exactly nothing.

Thirdly, the fact that organic molecules are present in meteorites is not an indication that there is life elsewhere in the universe. All of these molecules may be accounted for by a non-biological origin.

Fourthly, why haven't we detected extra-terrestrial life forms falling on us? More particularly, why wasn't life of some sort detected on Mars? Indeed, if Hoyle were correct, one would expect the moon and Mars to be knee-deep in bacteria, viruses and other organic debris.

Finally, and probably the most damning argument, Hoyle is unable to offer any explanation for how life arose in cometary material other than a version of the primeval soup scenario.

Diseases from space?

In his book *Diseases from Space* (1979), Hoyle extends his theory to propound the view that viruses and other micro-organisms are now falling on the earth giving rise to all forms of disease including AIDS, Legionnaire's disease, influenza and so on.

This is a modification of what seems a more reasonable scenario, namely that space-derived chemicals (or other such factors, such as an unidentified type of radiation) may trigger off viral genes contained within our own genome. I suspect he may have abandoned this because it would not have led him into the much more contentious field of evolution.

The concept of diseases from space has been propped up by the fact that bacteria do appear to be able to survive in a non-terrestrial environment. For instance, the organism *Streptococcus mitis* is supposed to have survived for two years within a T.V. camera left on the moon in 1967. Furthermore, Hoyle has dug out epidemiological evidence, such as the incidence of influenza in Eton College, that he believes supports his argument. In addition, he has tried to connect the occurrence of influenza epidemics with Halley's Comet. He has put forward the notion that the tail of this comet is one mass of microorganisms that descend upon the earth as it passes by.

Many of Hoyle's arguments are extremely naïve. If bacteria did occur in comets, one would expect them to be anaerobic, because of the lack of oxygen. How then can we explain aerobic bacteria? Furthermore, Hoyle's use of epidemiology to support his case is dubious. Epidemiology may be used to prove exactly what one would like to see. This is particularly so with a disease like influenza. It is much more likely that the observed distribution of influenza, in the cases quoted by Hoyle, has a far simpler explanation.

If viral diseases originate in outer space, how is it that a disease like rabies may be kept out of the United Kingdom by quarantine restrictions?

Furthermore, as viruses are uniquely adapted to replicate in avian and mammalian cells, one is left wondering how they replicate in outer space. And finally, how do viruses manage to descend to earth through space while being continuously exposed to intense ultra-violet radiation? For it is this same ultra-violet radiation which is used on earth to destroy viruses.

Evolution from space?

Taking his argument one step further, Hoyle has proposed that not only do viruses and bacteria rain down upon our heads from outer space, but also strange genes, which if they become incorporated into the genome of terrestrial organisms cause mutation. It is this mutation which Hoyle believes is the driving force for evolution. This theory is contained in the books *Evolution from Space* (1981) and *From Grains to Bacteria* (1984).

Hoyle uses these books for an attack on orthodox evolutionary theory, a task of no mean difficulty. He then proceeds to propose his own view of evolution in which cosmic genes are incorporated into earthly organisms. This, he argues, accounts for all the problems of conventional Darwinism. In particular, the sudden appearance of new species is explained; and the gaps in the fossil record now record occasions when a new gene appeared from space. It also explains neatly why there is convergent evolution, for instance, the eye of the octopus is, more or less, identical to that of the mammalian eye. Could both organisms at some time in the past have incorporated the same 'eye' gene? Such a proposition is not altogether far-fetched. If we take another instance of convergent evolution, that of the structural use of calcium phosphate, we find that this occurred in different phyla at approximately the same period. A. E. Mourant in a report in the journal *Nature* in 1971 (p.466) suggested that this was due to interaction with one viral gene that gave the necessary enzymes.

Yet there are many serious criticisms of Hoyle's ideas. Firstly, and probably the most serious, his theory doesn't explain the ultimate origin of life. It simply shifts the origin from the earth to space. How it started in that location is no clearer than how it began on earth.

Secondly, although genetic engineers are quite good at implanting genes into certain organisms, the likelihood that this could occur spontaneously with extra-terrestrial genes is implausible.

Thirdly, viruses, even if they did originate in interstellar space, could not be the original life form, as all viruses known today require energy and the translation mechanisms of existing cells in order to reproduce. Hoyle sees viruses as a precursor form of life, which every biologist knows to be nonsense.

Finally, probably the most absurd aspect of Hoyle's theory is the suggestion that genes may be formed *de novo* in space. Is he thinking of a sort of biological continuous creation? If so, he should think again.

Hoyle — a Daniel?

Although Hoyle has received considerable disdain from the scientific community, which has largely been justified, nevertheless, because of his reputation his ideas have received widespread circulation and discussion both within and outside the scientific community. Even the Royal Society took note and organized a seminar on the impact of cosmochemistry on terrestrial biology some time in 1981. Hoyle has also been able to lecture on his theories at various institutions. On one occasion during September 1980 he lectured to influenza experts at the National Institute of Biological Standards in London. Like Daniel in the lion's den he survived, but more for reasons British than biblical. One expert later commented that if he had been in America he would have been 'eaten alive'. [5] However, even after all this public attention, his ideas have failed to be taken up seriously by biologists. Some have attacked him with personal abuse, like the report in *Nature* which likened Hoyle and his collaborator to 'two kamikaze pilots proclaiming evolution from space directed by a cosmic intelligence from South Wales'. [6] Some individuals have even resorted to physical threats, such as the threat Hoyle's collaborator received from a mysterious Darwinist organization to burn his home to the ground.

I believe that Hoyle has made a most important contribution to science at this crucial stage in its history. From his retirement in the hills of Cumbria he has brought out into the open the problem concerning the origin of life on earth that previously there seemed a conspiracy not to discuss. Using his unique position he has broadcast from the BBC, written letters to the *Daily Telegraph* and published innumerable books informing us that the primeval soup theory is one gigantic myth. Let us conclude with his own words on this: 'It is remarkable that over the past half-century the scientific world has, almost without exception, believed a theory for which there is not a single supporting fact.' [7]

11. Is there extra-terrestrial life?

The origin of life is closely connected to one other major issue: namely, are we alone in the universe? In recent years this subject has excited man's imagination more than probably any other scientific issue. One need only recall the success of the film *E.T.* to appreciate how deep-rooted is man's need to believe he is not alone in the cosmos.

The idea that there were other inhabited planets goes back to the ancient Greeks. Plutarch tells us that Alexander, after conquering the then known world, wept on being told by the philosopher Anaxarchus that there were yet other inhabited worlds to subdue. However, Aristotle produced a series of rational arguments for a finite universe with a unique earth which became the accepted wisdom throughout late antiquity and right up to the Middle Ages.

The idea that the earth was just one of a series of planets surrounding the sun developed from the Copernican revolution. This led eventually to the concept of universal similitude, that is, the existence of many worlds. This became in a short time a firm principle of thought regarding the nature of the universe.

Thus in the seventeenth century the moon was imagined to be populated by lunar people. In Donne's *Ignatius his Conclave* published in 1611 we even find a proposal to establish a church on the moon. And in Kepler's *Somnium,* which was published posthumously in 1634, we find a fascinating description of the people who inhabit the far side of the moon. In 1638 Godwin, Bishop of Llandaff, published a romance about the lunar inhabitants.

By the close of the seventeenth century space travel, and particularly encounters with extra-terrestrials, became a popular theme for writers. Thus pluralism became the dominant outlook of scientists during the past four centuries. Sir David Brewster (1781–1868), the famous Scottish physicist, was a typical nineteenth-century pluralist believing that it would have been wasteful of a Creator not to populate the universe throughout with intelligent beings. There were, however, some voices of discontent. William Whewell, Master of Trinity College, Cambridge, broke with the prevailing pluralist view and created a heated controversy in 1853. He argued that geological evidence for man's appearance late in terrestrial history could be used to dismiss the pluralist case. He went further and denounced the astronomical evidence, claiming that the pluralists had jumped to too many assumptions. Yet Lord Kelvin wrote in 1872 that 'We all confidently believe that there are . . . many worlds of life besides our own.'[1]

Just how eager people are to believe in extra-terrestrial life is best illustrated by the famous 'Moon Hoax' incident of the early nineteenth century. The *New York Sun* newspaper in a desperate attempt to increase circulation engaged one Richard Adams Locke (1800-1871) to perpetrate a hoax concerning the discovery of life on the moon, supposedly by the English astronomer John Herschel. A huge sensation resulted so that the *Sun* soon became the best-selling newspaper in the world!

People have not changed. Look, for instance, at the vast numbers of people who take UFOs seriously. And even among scientists there have been many who seriously believed until recently that some form of life existed on Mars.

Most people are uncomfortable at the thought that we might be totally alone in the universe. Accordingly even today many intelligent people accept the likelihood of intelligent life outside our own planet.

One thing, however, most scientists are certain about, and that is that there is no life in our solar system other than our own. At one time it was popular for science fiction authors to speculate that life might be possible in the liquid ammonia oceans on Jupiter. This is now thought to be impossible for the reason that ammonia remains liquid over a very narrow temperature range of 44 degrees, compared to water, which is liquid for a hundred degrees Celsius. Furthermore, for it to remain liquid it must not rise above about $-40°C$, that is about $60°$ below the normal temperature on earth. For life to originate spontaneously under these conditions would require at least 1000 times the length of time postulated for life to have developed on earth, which would make it far older than the total age of the universe.

On the other hand, if life on earth was seeded from another world somewhere else in our galaxy, could not life have been seeded similarly in Jupiter? Again this is impossible because our form of life, based on water chemistry, could not have developed at those low temperatures. And furthermore, as seen from our previous argument, life anywhere else in the universe could not have developed based on ammonia chemistry (cf. Chapter 2).

Yet could life, having different chemical and physical properties from our own, have developed and evolved intelligence? Two sorts of suggestions have been made: a solid, inert form of life, or maybe a gaseous life form existing for a fraction of a second, in the sun for instance. Indeed Herschel believed that there may have been a form of life in the sun and this suggestion has recently been revived by Crick.

Although most of these suggestions remain in the realm of science fiction, the extrapolation of the concept has been seriously entertained by some eminent scientists. J. D. Bernal, for instance, believed it might one day be possible to interbreed life from different parts of the universe producing, to use his own words, 'a kind of superlife . . .'[2] Pink spiders no doubt! The question regarding extra-terrestrial life is therefore the ultimate extension of permissory materialism.

Argument for extra-terrestrial life

Many scientists today will assure us that advanced intelligent civilizations exist scattered about our galaxy. On what do they base this conclusion?

Their argument is extremely simple, if naïve. It runs along these lines: our sun is an average star. A planet (Earth) rich in life is in orbit around it. In our galaxy, alone, there are about 100,000 million other stars. Many of these are identical in age and brightness to the sun. Thus the probability of any of those stars also having a planet similar to the earth works out to be between 200,000 and 800 million. Even if we take the lower figure and assume it is out by a factor of a hundred, this still leaves 2000 planets like earth on which life will have started. All right, some life will not have reached the stage of that on earth but there must be several hundred with life more advanced than our own. If we extend this argument to all the other galaxies in the universe one arrives at the conclusion that the universe must be littered with advanced forms of life.

This argument is very convincing. Its fallacy, however, is that we cannot assume that all other stars will have a planetary system like our own. In fact, the only evidence that some stars may have planets is from distortion of the Doppler effect. But this might well have another explanation, so it is a dangerous line of reasoning to base everything on this one observation. There is no other evidence that any other star in the cosmos has a planetary system. And even if unequivocal evidence for other planets were obtained, it would be an unacceptable step to then assume that they could foster life. Until we know how life arose on earth we cannot even speculate with any certainty that there could be life on other planets.All speculation in the past has been based on trust in the primeval soup scenario which we now know to be false.

Communication with extra-terrestrial life

Proof for extra-terrestrial life would follow if direct communication were to be made with it. This subject thirty years ago would have been laughable, yet today the climate is such that it is treated with deadly seriousness and has become part of modern science. Most people have come across the abbreviations: SETI meaning *S*earch for *E*xtra-*T*errestrial *I*ntelligence; and CETI, standing for *C*ommunication with *E*xtra-*T*errestrial *I*ntelligence. The first serious discussion regarding SETI took place in 1959. During the next decade the search for extra-terrestrial life became one of the top priorities of the United States space programme on which many millions of dollars were expended. One is amazed that so much public money could be spent on SETI, which is very much on the edge of scientific respectability, whereas hardly anything is spent on other fringe areas such as parapsychology.

Attempts to communicate with extra-terrestrial life go back to the last century, when in 1817 the German astronomer Karl Friedrich Gauss suggested that strips of Siberian forest be laid out into geometric shapes so that they could be recognized by intelligent beings on other planets. One suggestion was to use the shape representing Pythagoras' Theorem. Not long after this the French scientist Charles Cros urged his government to construct huge mirrors to reflect sunlight towards Mars and thereby send messages in semaphore to the Martians.

Some time after the Great War the Sperry Gyroscope Company proposed that its new high-powered searchlights should be used to beam light towards Mars. Although this idea was not adopted, in the August of the year 1924, as Mars made a close approach to earth, the Chief of Operations in the U.S. Navy ordered twenty of his most powerful communications centres to cease transmission so that they could listen for any Martian radio signals.

In our own time we have again witnessed how seriously some scientists take the possibility of communicating with extra-terrestrials. When Pioneer 10 was launched by NASA on 3 March 1972 it had on its side a small gold-anodized aluminium plate that had been added on somewhat as an afterthought in what Isaac Asimov has called 'a matter of sheer bravado'. The plaque, designed by Carl Sagan, shows a naked man and woman. The man has his right hand raised in the traditional American greeting. Near the bottom of the plate is a diagram, by Sagan's wife, Linda Salzman, of the solar system with an arrow indicating that the spacecraft had originated from the planet Earth. The fact that the officials at NASA thought it worthwhile putting this plaque on the spacecraft, and indeed later on Pioneer 11, indicates the seriousness with which the subject is viewed. It would seem that even scientists are allowed to have castles in the sky.

E.T. — a pipe-dream?

Enrico Fermi, the physicist, on being presented with the usual mathematical argument for a large number of other civilizations in the universe, raised the obvious question: 'Where is everybody?'[3]

This simple point of view has led to a transformation in scientific attitudes. Let us examine what Fermi is getting at.

I can remember as a youngster in the early 1950s reading in a newspaper an article about artificial satellites. All science fiction, we concluded, but how wrong we were! Within a couple of years one could see them in the sky and within two decades a man had been put on the moon. Since that time we have had a space vehicle land on the Martian soil and seen remarkable pictures of most of the outer planets on our television screens. All this in one lifetime. If we don't have a global nuclear war, or a new disease doesn't kill us all off, what could be achieved in a hundred years' time? A thousand years' time? Or even a million years' time? Such a period of time is but a blink of the eye in relation to the theoretical age of the universe.

It would seem logical to suppose that man would find some way of travelling to distant stars in the expectation of inhabiting new and distant planets. In other words, in a very short period, the human species would be expected to colonize the universe.

If there are, however, many thousands, possibly millions, of other earth-like planets having more advanced civilizations than ourselves, then they should by now have reached earth. *But they haven't,* which is strong *prima facie* evidence that all those theoretical civilizations are simply not there!

James Trefil, Professor of Physics at the University of Virginia, has concluded that this sort of logical argument has 'convinced many members of the scientific community that the optimistic estimates of the abundance of extra-terrestrial life bandied about in the 1960s and 1970s were simply wrong'.[4]

Dr Reinhard Brener, in his book *Contact with the Stars: The Search for Extra-terrestrial Life* (Freeman, 1982), has gone even further. He presents a view that is becoming the new orthodoxy in science, namely that the origin and development of life is not as simplistic as was thought during the 1960s and that we might very well be a unique feature of our galaxy.

One reason for this change in direction results from the pioneering work of Michael Hart on the development of planetary atmospheres. Hart has proposed that the factors that influence early atmospheres, such as vulcanism, and life itself, result in a finely balanced system, the equilibrium of which may easily be destabilized. If this occurs a greenhouse effect may result, so making the planet too hot for life to exist, as is the case with Venus; or it may become too cold and end up a frozen ball, like Mars and Titan.

The general conclusion is best summarized by Professor James Trefil in a review in *Nature* (1982): 'As I write this, watching my daughters playing in the surf at Cape Hatteras, it is hard to imagine that everything I see — the clouds, the people, the ocean itself — is the result of a happy set of chance occurrences that are unlikely to have been repeated elsewhere. *Yet that is precisely what the past 20 years of research on the origins of life tells us.*'[5]

Many others now accept the impossibility of intelligent extra-terrestrials. Even the science fiction writer Harry Harrison has reluctantly concluded concerning the probability argument for extra-terrestrial life that: 'At its best this is wishful thinking, at its worst just guesswork. It won't do. I, like most people, would like to think that we are not alone in the universe. But that is just a hope unsupported by biological evidence.'[6]

In conclusion, the concept of plurality of worlds is an intellectual position adopted by those not fettered to any religion and so free to build castles in the sky. If extra-terrestrial intelligent life were to be discovered next week one cannot deny that it would create difficult theological problems. However, these would be insignificant compared to our need to protect ourselves from alien beings that would almost certainly be much more sophisticated than ourselves.

Most intelligent people today would do well to forget the pipedream of the existence of extra-terrestrial life and accept the earth's singularity. If other similar planets do exist outside our galaxy then they will for ever remain lost to us, as did God's alternative worlds in mediaeval philosophy. As Professor Stanley Jaki, a Benedictine priest, has concluded in his book *Cosmos and Creator* (1981), extra-terrestrial life is the ultimate extension of Darwinism and an utterly self-defeating exercise in wishful thinking.

12. Evidence for how life began

Most scientists today find the need to invoke a final cause anathema. Yet, in any investigation if the evidence points to something are we right in dismissing it simply because it is unfashionable?

Let us therefore take that step, not in faith, but purely on scientific grounds, and accept some act of creation. The crucial question must be 'At what stage do we invoke a Creator?' As I have remarked in the previous chapter, the idea of a benevolent Creator who would permit life to evolve by blind chance appears a contradiction. Surely, one may just as easily propose an act of creation *in toto*. Such a stance, although it would currently be odious, is nonetheless logically far more reasonable, being a statement of the obvious. Let us therefore put our hypothesis to the test as one would any other scientific hypothesis. Accordingly one would expect it to fulfil two important criteria, namely:

1. It must enable predictions to be made, some of which must be verifiable.

2 . It should explain and unify data that previously was isolated and fragmented.

Let us look at each of these in turn. Firstly, can we make any prediction from our hypothesis? I believe we may. We ought to be able to find evidence for intelligent design, very much as Paley recognized and persuasively argued for in his classic work of apology.

Paley looked at the natural world and saw evidence for intelligent design and contrivance. 'Where there is design,' he argued, 'there must be a designer and where there is contrivance there must be a contriver.' At the time he put forward this argument, around the beginning of the nineteenth century, his logic was impeccable. However, in the second half of the century the Darwinian revolution attributed the work of the great designer to the blind forces of natural selection and Paley's argument was generally believed to have been refuted.

Today, however, we are able to apply Paley's argument not to the world about us, but at a microscopic level, in particular to the subcellular molecular world. If we can discover evidence for design then, unlike Paley's case, it cannot be refuted, because there is no evidence that the cell has actually evolved. We simply do not know of any life except that based on cells. Nor is there any evidence that a sub-cellular form of life has ever existed.

I believe molecular biology now reveals evidence for intelligent design. This conclusion is based on the following:

1. The nature of the genetic code.

2. The existence of molecules of perfection.

3. The unusual structures of the pigments of life.

4. The complexity of gene structure.

5. The precise structural features of enzymes.

Let us look in detail at the inferences we may make from the above.

The genetic code

We have already discussed in chapter 6 the difficulties that surround any explanation for the origin of the genetic code. Crick has presented a substantial case for the code's not having arisen spontaneously. He argued as follows: 'The important point to realize is that in spite of the genetic code being almost universal, the mechanism necessary to embody it is far too complex for it to have arisen in one blow.'[1]

I have already argued that it could not have arisen from a simpler system. Furthermore it seems inconceivable that the code originated as a triplet code and then underwent subsequent refinement. But if one rules out evolution of the code by way of a slow refinement and its only alternative — spontaneous formation — then what is one left with? The solution, I believe, rests with a detailed scrutiny.

The genetic code we find today in all organisms is programmed to incorporate only twenty amino acids. Yet there are sixty-four possible code words. Why are only twenty amino acids incorporated into proteins? At this point we discover an intriguing enigma. For in fact, contrary to what most elementary textbooks would have us believe, many proteins contain amino acids other than the twenty coded for by the genetic code.

Take, for instance, the protein collagen. This protein is the most ubiquitous structural protein of both vertebrates and invertebrates. Collagen has been found to contain at least two unusual amino acids, namely, 4-hydroxy proline and 5-hydroxy lysine. These amino acids are essential for the structural and functional integrity of the protein. Indeed it is difficult to envisage collagen existing without them. Yet these amino acids are not coded for in the genetic code. They are produced in the protein after it has been manufactured. Specific enzymes are needed to introduce hydroxy groups into both proline and lysine residues of the protein chain.

PROLINE   4-HYDROXY-PROLINE

Many other proteins also contain unusual amino acids. Gamma carboxy-glutamic acid is present in certain bone proteins where it is essential in binding calcium. Methylated and acetylated amino acids are found in histone proteins, where they play a vital role.

As one might expect almost all of these amino acids to occur in the primeval soup, why are they not represented by specific codons? The necessity to rely on particular enzymes to effect the post-translation modification is surely disadvantageous, particularly with forty-four codons going spare. One would have expected some of these 'unusual' amino acids to be coded for, but none are.

Extrapolating this argument further, I would conclude that the availability of forty-four spare codons is highly significant. In particular, I believe it could not have come about by blind chance but by an act of deliberate contrivance. For a degenerate genetic code has the overall effect of minimizing harmful mutations. One would not expect this to be so if the genetic code had arisen by blind chance.

To illustrate what I mean let us consider the amino acid alanine. This amino acid is coded for by the codons GCU, GCC, GCA and GCG. It can immediately be seen that only the first two letters are essential. Therefore regardless of which base is in the third position only alanine will be coded for. This is what is meant by code degeneracy. Accordingly, if there were to be a mutation in the third position, let us say, the sequence GCU was mistakenly copied as GCC, then alanine would still be incorporated into the protein and although a mutation had occurred there would be no harmful consequences.

The incorporation of an incorrect amino acid into a protein may on occasions have quite lethal consequences. Probably the best illustration of this is that of the abnormal human haemoglobins. Here a single mutation gives rise to the fatal disease known as sickle cell anaemia which is found in individuals largely of African descent. The abnormal haemoglobin known as HbS results from a single mutation when a glutamic acid is replaced by a valine. When we look at the appropriate codons we find glutamic acid is coded for by GAA and valine GUA. When the mutation occurs the middle base A is replace by U. Thus, just one incorrect base out of 861 causes this lethal disease.

But such mutations are extremely rare because the genetic code in all living organisms minimizes the rate of mutation. This is contrary to what one would expect if the genetic code had arisen by blind chance. Furthermore, and even more significantly, if the genetic code had come about spontaneously and by chance, then one would have expected it to be a doublet code and not a triplet code as we find it.

A doublet genetic code would have permitted the incorporation of only sixteen amino acids. But this would have been perfectly adequate to construct most proteins needed for life. With a doublet code *every* mutation would have resulted in a changed protein. Mutation rates would have been extremely rapid, so permitting evolution to proceed at a much faster pace. If life is the result of blind chance, one would certainly have expected a genetic code having codons of two bases and not three. The fact that this is not so indicates a designing purpose behind what we now see as the genetic code.

Molecules of perfection

Vitamin B_{12} is one of the most complex natural substances known. It is constructed around a corrin ring system, which resembles the porphyrin ring, as found in haemoglobin. In addition to this unique feature the coenzyme B_{12} contains a most unusual carbon to cobalt bond. These substances exhibit what I have come to term 'molecular perfection'.

When William Paley looked at the human eye he argued that it was so perfect in its construction that it must have been purposely designed. Similarly at a molecular level vitamin B_{12} is so perfect in its construction that it too exhibits evidence of design. The evolutionist, however, will argue that vitamin B_{12} has evolved via a large number of precursors, each of which had a lesser role to play in metabolism. But where are they? If they had existed in the past, surely there would be some trace evident in the many millions of organisms that populate the earth today. So far none have been found. This very fact indicates to me that they have never existed.

That vitamin B_{12} is not the product of an evolutionary process may readily be proved by the following argument.

Today we find that vitamin B_{12}, although essential for all life, is only manufactured by certain micro-organisms. Humans, for instance, require about 1 μgm of it each day. Without this we become ill and eventually die. This daily requirement is obtained from our diet: eggs, for example, contain about 0.7 μgm/100 gms, and milk around 0.3 μgm/100 gms. But in all instances the vitamin found its way into these foodstuffs ultimately from micro-organisms, usually intestinal microbes. Surprisingly even higher plants are also unable to synthesize this vitamin.

Vitamin B_{12}'s role is as a co-enzyme. It participates in many reactions, particularly in the biosynthesis of nucleotides and so is vital for DNA synthesis. Without it most organisms would perish.

The evolutionist's argument is that the precursor of plants and animals lost the ability to make vitamin B_{12} around one billion years ago, when life had reached the eukaroytic level. Furthermore, the evolutionist will assume that the biosynthesis of vitamin B_{12} itself developed over about two billion years, that is from the primeval soup to the first organism. Once vitamin B_{12} had formed presumably its evolution then stopped. Accordingly its structure has remained static during the subsequent billion years. Why did its evolution stop?

The only acceptable explanation is that it is a molecule perfectly formed for its function. It is therefore a molecule of perfection. But if the evolutionist is right, there should not be such a thing. Chance only produces molecules at random and these should continually change with time. Vitamin B_{12} should not have remained static over billions of years. Yet no evolutionist in his right mind is going to suggest that this complex organic substance could have formed spontaneously in the primeval soup.

Where does this leave us? Vitamin B_{12} is a molecule perfectly designed for its role in life. It could not have formed by chance in any primeval soup. Its existence and distribution in nature can only indicate intelligent and purposeful design.

FIGURE 10
The complex molecular structure of vitamin B12

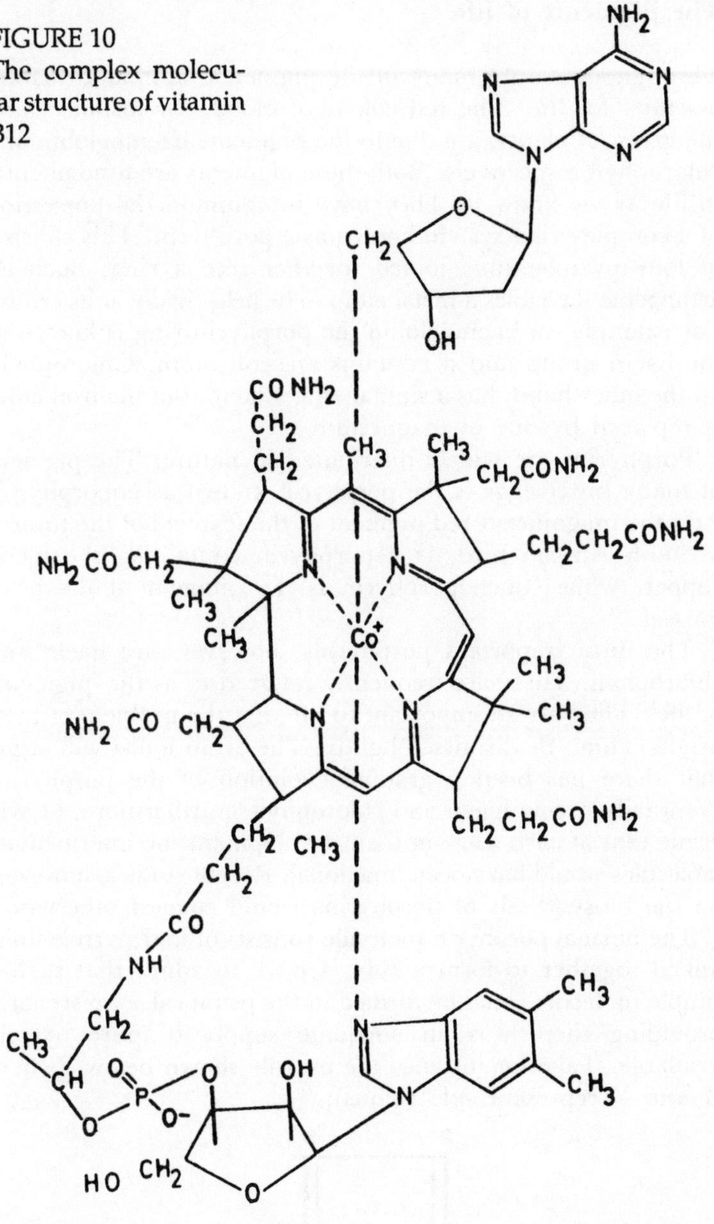

The pigments of life

Throughout nature many of the pigments familiar to us are essential for life. The red colour of blood, for instance, and the green of plants, are due to the pigments haemoglobin and chlorophyll respectively. Both these pigments are fundamental to life as we know it. They have in common the possession of a complex ring system known as a porphyrin. This consists of four pyrrole units joined together into a ring. Such an arrangement enables a metal atom to be held rigidly at its centre. For example, in haemoglobin the porphyrin ring is known as the haem group and it contains an iron atom. Chlorophyll, on the other hand, has a similar ring system, but the iron atom is replaced by one of magnesium.

Porphyrins are widely distributed in nature. The pigment of many birds' eggs is the porphyrin known as ooporphyrin. And the magnificent red pigment of the feathers of the turaco, a South African bird, is a porphyrin containing the metal copper, while conchoporphyrin is the pigment of the pearl mussel.

The most important porphyrins, however, are haem and chlorophyll. These are frequently referred to as the 'pigments of life'. They are so important to life that the problem of their origin cannot be dismissed lightly. The evolutionist will argue that there has been a gradual evolution of the porphyrins eventually giving haem and chlorophyll. Furthermore, he will argue that at each stage in their development the intermediate molecules would have been functional. Recent studies, however, on the biosynthesis of porphyrins would suggest otherwise.

The normal porphyrin molecule consists of four pyrrole units linked together to form a ring. I have to admit that such a simple molecule could be formed in the primeval soup scenario providing there was an adequate supply of pure pyrrole available. Take for instance the pyrrole shown below, (where X and Y represent side chains):

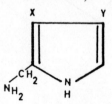

Under certain circumstances this may undergo spontaneous polymerization to give the porphyrin:

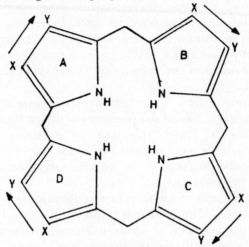

Now it is important here to see that the side chains X and Y rotate around the ring in a clockwise direction.

The enigmatic problem is that in all natural porphyrins the side chains attached to pyrrole D face the opposite direction, thus:

We now know from studies on the biosynthesis of the porphyrin ring systems of haemoglobin, the cytochromes and chlorophyll, that two discrete enzymes are needed to convert a pyrrole into the porphyrin uroporphyrinogen III, which is the most important first step. One of these enzymes is known as cosynthetase and it is this enzyme that causes the complex rearrangement of the orientation of the side chains contained in pyrrole D. [2]

The reason why this complex rearrangement is needed is still a mystery. Yet all the pigments of life go through this process. This fact clearly rules out the possibility that the first pigments of life were formed by chance, for before they could be made the existence of the enzyme cosynthetase would have been a prerequisite.

The pigments of life therefore could not have originated by blind chance. Their strange biosynthetic pathway indicates quite clearly the presence of an overall designing principle.

This brings us to consider the origin of biosynthetic pathways. The evolutionists argue that the first organisms were heterotrophic, that is they were unable to manufacture any of the substances needed for life but obtained them directly from the primeval soup. As time went on the essential substances ran out. Under these circumstances a mutant organism able to synthesize a vital nutrient survived while all the others perished. Hence the biosynthetic pathways evident to us today. To illustrate this further let us take a particular example, namely the amino acid tryptophan. This is a vital amino acid for many proteins and almost all enzymes. Its biosynthesis requires ten precursor molecules. Now according to the evolutionist's argument, all these precursors must also have been present in the primeval soup. Thus when supplies of tryptophan were exhausted, that organism able to convert precursor one (Pre_1) into tryptophan survived and the remainder perished. When supplies of Pre_1 ran out, only those organisms possessing the enzymes to convert precursor two (Pre_2) into Pre_1, and Pre_1 into tryptophan survived, and so on. This is summarized in the diagram on page 137.

FIGURE 11

Hypothetical evolution of the biosynthesis of the amino acid tryptophan

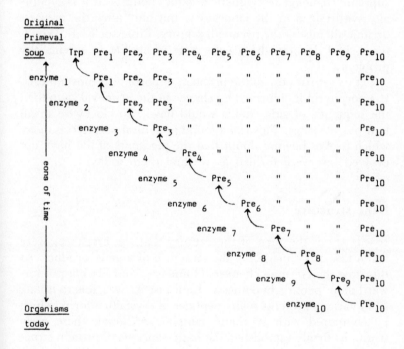

Thus, at the end of the day, the only organisms able to survive were those possessing the entire repertoire of enzymes needed to form tryptophan, from simple precursors as is found today in autotrophic organisms.

But such an argument is absurd, for it implies that complex biochemicals, such as vitamin B_{12}, not only were formed spontaneously in the primeval soup but all their intermediate precursors also. This is complete madness. It is difficult enough to see how a simple molecule such as tryptophan could have formed by chance in the primeval soup, let alone one as complex as vitamin B_{12}. This molecule for many years represented the supreme challenge to synthetic organic chemists. It was eventually synthesized in the laboratory, but only after the greatest organic chemist of the twentieth century, Professor R. B. Woodward, had devoted the greater part of his life to solving the problem.

Let us return now to the problem of porphyrin biosynthesis. If a porphyrin had formed by chance in the primeval soup then the sequence of side chains would have run clockwise in all four pyrrole rings. This is not found in natural porphyrins today which proves beyond doubt that the pigments of life have not evolved but were formed as we find them today.

Gene structure

It was about the turn of the century that the first steps were taken towards elucidating the structure of a gene product. At this time the German chemists Hofmeister and Fischer put forward their 'peptide hypothesis'. Emil Fischer was able to isolate from various proteins many peptides in crystalline form, which he compared with synthetic samples. Although these early triumphs firmly established the basic concepts of protein structure, it was clear that the methods of classical organic chemistry were quite inadequate. Fifty years were to elapse before any further progress was made. By that time the techniques of paper chromatography and electrophoresis had been introduced. It was using these methods that Frederick Sanger was able to determine the complete amino acid sequence of insulin in 1955. This was the culmination of a decade of work by Sanger. Looking back, one might point out that his choice of insulin, a small protein of fifty-one amino acids, was fortunate. If he had chosen a larger protein, for instance haemoglobin, having 574 amino acids, the work could very well still be in progress, if not abandoned many years ago. Sanger's achievement must surely rank as one of the great landmarks in science this century, as it provided the proof that proteins did indeed have unique structures and could be regarded as definite molecules and not simply as vague colloids. The development of the genetic code was a direct consequence of Sanger's work and subsequently led to the advent of the new science of molecular biology. Once started this science expanded at a phenomenal rate, furthermore, new techniques were introduced that enabled many more structures to be determined. Yet because of the degeneracy of the genetic code, it was not possible to infer the structure of a gene simply from a protein sequence. This only became possible when in the late 1960s techniques were introduced, again largely by Frederick Sanger, actually to sequence genes.

It was using such techniques that Pierre Chambon of the Louis Pasteur University in Strasburg made the startling discovery that genes did not invariably consist of a continuous sequence of nucleotides. He discovered that genes were usually split into sections separated by what has been called 'nonsense' DNA. These are now referred to as 'introns' and the protein-forming sections as 'exons'.

It is now well established that in all higher organisms the protein-coding genes are made of exons and the intervening regions, the introns, are not translated into protein. Let us look at what this means for a protein like myoglobin.

Myoglobin consists largely of helical segments of peptide chain folded up into a compact structure leaving a cleft into which the haem group fits just like a coin entering a slot.

The gene for this protein consists of three exons separated by very long introns as shown below:

FIGURE 12   The myoglobin gene

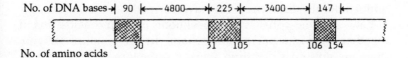

No. of DNA bases → 90 |← 4800 →|← 225 →|← 3400 →| 147 |←

No. of amino acids   30   31   105   106 154

The central exon, coding for amino acids 31–105, is responsible for that region of the protein that binds to the haem group. But the other two exons are also essential in providing protein regions that ensure that the amino acids that bind to the haem group have the precise orientation.

The evolutionist will argue that myoglobin evolved from a precursor consisting solely of residues 31–105 and that the other sections were added on in refinement. But this ignores the fact that experimental testing of the central region alone in binding haem has proved unsuccessful. In fact, all the three regions are necessary for full activity of the protein. So how could such a complicated arrangement have arisen? It is simply too unnecessarily complicated to have arisen by blind chance. It would be equivalent to forecasting that rain would fall in Manchester *only* on the following days: 5, 6 and 7 January, 12–21 June and 16–19 December, out of an entire year. Clearly impossible!

The mechanisms needed to enable the selection of random, and disconnected, sequences in this way are too complex to have arisen by chance. It would have demanded the pre-existence of highly sophisticated mechanisms for the selection of appropriate exon regions from the vast number of possible permutations. Even so, it would have been a painfully slow process, incompatible with the basic assumptions of Darwinism. One may conclude therefore that our present understanding of gene structure speaks out loud and clear for intelligent design, *not* evolution.

The precise structural features of enzymes

All life as we know it is ultimately dependent upon enzyme molecules. Enzymes are therefore a prerequisite for life. But as enzymes are only found in, and associated with, living cells, how could the first enzymes have formed?

Each enzyme consists of a backbone of amino acids linked together, giving a polypeptide chain. In the smallest enzyme there are around 120 amino acids, but the largest enzyme may contain more than a thousand. Along this chain will be positioned about six crucial amino acids, so that when the peptide chain is folded up they come together forming the so-called 'active-site'. This is the enzyme's power-house.

It is possible to demonstrate by simple mathematics that the 2000 or so enzymes necessary for life could not have been formed by random chance. The argument runs as follows: using the twenty normal amino acids, then the number of different combinations for 2000 enzyme-like chains with six different amino‐acids in the active site would be about $10^{13,000}$.

The probability of finding all these at any particular time as a chance arrangement is therefore one in $10^{13,000}$, in other words, an immensely unlikely event. Just to illustrate the enormity of this number, consider some of the following:

the number of atoms in the entire universe is 10^{80};

the number of milliseconds in 4 billion years is 10^{54}; and

the number of stars in the unverse is about 10^{22}.

Without enzymes there could be no life, but without life there are no enzymes. If the enzymes needed for life could not have arisen spontaneously, as the above calculation indicates, then they must have come about by creative design. The necessity of so many enzymes coming together to give life is unequivocal proof that life was brought about following an act of creation. Accordingly, enzymes have not evolved by a process of gradual change, but are perfectly designed to carry out their specified tasks.

The above examples serve to demonstrate design at a subcellular level and so fulfil the first criterion for our hypothesis as defined at the beginning of this chapter. Let us now continue and demonstrate that the creation theory is also able to explain and unify data that previously was isolated, confusing and fragmented. I believe there are four main criteria that reveal this.

1. It offers a solution to the puzzling molecular interrelationships that have been recently discovered at a sub-cellular level.

2. It gives a more plausible explanation of why certain species lack particular traits.

3. It accounts for the demonstrable lack of intermediate biologies that one finds in nature.

4. It explains the lack of diversity that is found at a subcellular level.

Let us examine each of these in turn.

1. Explaining molecular interrelationships
Firstly, convincing evidence for creation is to be found in the recognition of molecular interrelationships that exist at the subcellular level.

For several decades now it has been known that there exist in the central nervous system of man specific molecular receptors that bind plant-derived drugs, for instance, morphine. These receptors are highly specific for morphine, complementing its structure in a manner analogous to a lock and key. So perfect is this match that even relatively small changes in the structure of the morphine molecule result in a dramatic alteration in its pharmacological activity. [3]

The discovery of these specific receptors for plant-derived drugs in man poses the enigma why they are there. In particular, it drives the evolutionist into a tight corner whereupon he is forced to argue that these receptors have survived, apparently unused, throughout aeons of time. However, he cannot explain why they did not become selectively eliminated. What he expects us to believe is that these receptors were formed billions of years ago, long before plants diverged from animals. And during subsequent evolution they remained repressed in the gene pool only to reappear when man came on the scene. What spurious nonsense!

Surely it is more logical, and reasonable, to believe that their existence is indicative of an overall plan in nature? If this is not conclusive evidence for design, then nothing is.

Yet the evolutionist has more to contend with. For during the last few years there has been an avalanche of similar findings revealing a complex interrelationship at the sub-cellular level. Much of this has arisen from the large number of new protein sequences inferred from DNA studies. Among the vast body of data now available have come many surprising discoveries. Most remarkable has been the finding that many proteins of unrelated functions and from widely different species have almost identical sequences. Let us look at some of the wholly unexpected similarities.

First, there is the finding that the protein α-crystallin from the human eye lens has a strikingly similar structure to a small heat shock protein found in the fruit-fly *Drosophila*. Similar proteins in the human eye lens and an insect? What has the evolutionist to say about that? In fact, they have been remarkably silent. But there is more to come.

A protein PTTH (prothoracicotrophic hormone) found in certain insects, where it causes metamorphosis, is remarkably similar to human insulin! Even more surprising is the finding that insects have receptor molecules for mammalian insulin. Furthermore, a neuropeptide produced by certain Hydra is also made in the human hypothalamus. And many other human hormones have been found in micro-organisms. Thus there is an insulin-like protein in the fungus *Aspergillus fumigatus*. And the human hormones calcitonin, thyroid hormone and chorionic gonadotropin are found in the microbes *Escherichia coli* and *Clostridium perfringens*. Surprisingly, a protein very similar to human insulin has been discovered in spinach and a protein analogous to human interferon has been found in tobacco.

The evolutionist is at a loss to account for these remarkable findings, yet they are readily accounted for if one accepts that there is an overall design and plan in nature.

2. Are traits lost?

One of the fundamental problems in evolutionary biology is in explaining why disused traits become repressed and eventually genetically eliminated. Evolutionists point to instances where eyes have degenerated to become rudimentary, vestigial or have even disappeared altogether due to the adoption by the animal of a dark environment. For instance, the fish that live in the abyssal depths of the ocean, such as the teleost *Ipnops,* are completely blind, having no trace of eyes. Similarly, the cavernicolous fish *Noemacheilus smithi,* that is found in the deep caves of the Zagros Mountains of Iran, is blind and lacks eyes. The same is true of the cavernicolous salamander *Typhlomolge rathbuni,* which is found in subterranean streams and wells of Texas.

Darwin's explanation, which is still accepted today, is that a disused character still requires energy to build and so is selectively disadvantageous. Eventually selection will eliminate it so as to recoup the wasted cost in its construction. The cost, of course, is the biosynthetic energy needed for this construction.

The same argument may be used by evolutionists to explain why disused proteins and enzymes become phenotypically repressed and eventually genetically eliminated. However, this traditional explanation has recently been disproved by some elegant experiments conducted by D. E. Dykhuizen on certain mutants of the bacterium *Escherichia coli* and reported in the journal *Nature* for 5 June 1986. [4]

Furthermore, the saved-energy idea may easily be disproved by looking at a very familiar aspect of our daily life, namely the necessity to include vitamins in our diet.

Most vitamins needed by man for good health are also required by other species of animal. Vitamin A, for instance, is essential for bone development and for good vision, and the vitamins of the B complex play a variety of roles in maintaining good health. The evolutionist will argue that the precursor of all modern animals and man lost the ability to synthesize these vitamins early in the history of life on earth, most likely when our precursor began to live on plants, for these contain an abundance of vitamins. Thus just as the fish lost its eyes when it no longer needed them, so too did our ancestor when it no longer needed to manufacture these special nutrients.

The Darwinist would have us believe that the energy saved gave a selective advantage to our precursor animal. This argument is absurd. To demonstrate this let us look at two interesting problems associated with vitamins B_{12} and C. Firstly, vitamin B_{12}: as we have mentioned previously, this vitamin is required in very low concentrations. For instance, man requires about 1 μgm/day. Accordingly, can one seriously argue that the saved energy in making so little of a substance could have possibly given a selective advantage? The energy saved would be insignificant. If, as it is thought, the loss of capability to manufacture B_{12} occurred probably at the unicellular level, then the saved energy would have been inconsequential. On the other hand, as vitamin B_{12} is essential for all life, playing, as it does, an important role in the synthesis of DNA, how could it have been selectively advantageous to have lost the capacity to make it?

Let us now turn our attention to vitamin C (ascorbic acid).

In this case most species of animal, except the guinea pig, man and certain other primates, are able to manufacture it within their own tissues. However, this poses a particularly thorny problem for the evolutionist, namely, why didn't other mammals such as the cow, sheep and horse also lose their capacity to make this vitamin?

The Darwinist will claim that an animal will abandon its capacity to manufacture a vitamin if its diet is providing an unusually large surplus of it. Yet, from a knowledge of the vitamin C content of most natural foods one may calculate the approximate intake of vitamin C in any animal. Then if one extrapolates back to the alleged common ancestor of the mammalian species, one is forced to conclude that *all* modern mammals theoretically should have lost their capacity to make vitamin C. But this is not so.

The only conclusion one can reach is that the evolutionist's saved-energy hypothesis is wrong. If so, how can he account for lost traits? Did the cave salamander ever possess eyes? Did the blind fish ever see? And did our ancestor ever make vitamin C? The evolutionist has no satisfactory answer to these problems. Yet if our hypothesis of creation *in toto* is correct, there is no problem. Species appear to be as they were meant to be. Traits are not lost — they were never there in the first place!

3. Where are the intermediate biologies?
If life had evolved, then it must have done so via a progressive change in its biochemistry. Yet in all living organisms today there is no evidence for such a progression. In fact we find quite the reverse. Micro-organisms, which are frequently viewed as 'primitive' organisms on the evolutionary scale, have a far more complex biochemistry than do 'higher' organisms.

The Darwinist usually points to the vertebrate eye and persuades us to believe that it has evolved over millions of years. He then offers a kaleidoscopic view of its evolution by showing us primitive visual systems of molluscs and so on. Indeed, he might very well succeed in convincing many people that he is right.

But can he do the same at a sub-cellular level? Can he show us the progressive changes in enzyme structure? He might be able to show us half an eye, but can he show us half a ribosome?

No he cannot, for the biochemical organization of each organism is perfect in its own right.

The clear lack of biochemical progression is strong evidence against evolution. Surely it indicates that life was created very much as we see it today.

4. Why a lack of molecular diversity?

There is a remarkable lack of biochemical diversity. Indeed, the lack of diversity at a sub-cellular level indicates that either life arose by spontaneous generation only once, or that life was created.

We find that all scientists are agreed that life, no matter what form it takes, has the same basic biochemical and biophysical characteristics. Thus all enzymes appear to be constructed along similar principles, so that an enzyme from a bacterium may have an identical counterpart in man.

Furthermore, the mode of inheritance is uniform throughout nature, as is the genetic code. Proteins are constructed in all organisms by a similar mechanism and only the same twenty amino acids are employed from microbe to man. Similar metabolic pathways are employed in all creatures, large or small. Also chirality is uniform throughout the living world, and so one could go on.

Would one expect such a uniform pattern to emerge if life had evolved by blind chance? The Darwinist would reply that he would, for he accepts the basic tenet that life arose by spontaneous generation only *once*. Therefore, he would conclude that one would expect all creatures, from viruses, bacteria, plants and animals to be built on the same principles.

But is this a valid interpretation? The evolutionist recognizes that there is a uniformity in nature, therefore he concludes life must have had a unique origin. One could equally argue that because life is supported by the same principles, therefore it has been designed according to those rules. Both are equally valid.

However, the evolutionist's case may easily be demolished by posing the simple question: 'Why should life have had a single origin?'

If life could have arisen once by chance, why could not it have occurred twice, three times . . . and so on? Evolutionists conclude it has not done so because of the uniformity they find at the molecular level.

One many conclude from the fact that we do not see a diversity of form at the sub-cellular level that life must have originated by a unique event. This event could not have been the result of chance, but a deliberate act of creation.

13. Conclusion

In 1943 Erwin Schrödinger recognized that the introduction of new physical techniques in science was about to transform classical biology. The revolution he foresaw occurred shortly after publication of his book that posed the question, 'What is life?' Although this was a fundamental appraisal of the situation at that time he nevertheless avoided going as far as to ask, 'How did life originate?', for he knew the stage was not ready to tackle that question.

Today, almost half a century later, we are in possession of a wealth of scientific information that would have staggered even Schrödinger. Yet, naturalistic science is no nearer answering that question. In truth, its solution appears to be even more elusive.

Indeed, our knowledge of the living cell is such that instead of our being able to explain how life may have arisen from inanimate matter, each new discovery seems to chase the solution further and further away. So much so that many scientists are now reconciled to the belief that we never will find an explanation. Francis Crick has despaired of the situation and concluded: 'I cannot myself see just how we shall ever decide how life orginated.'[1] And the physicist Freeman Dyson, writing in his book *Origins of Life*, reaches almost halfway before making the remarkable statement: 'We know almost nothing about the origin of life.'[2]

Molecular biology has therefore not solved the problem of the origin of life; it has simply made the problem appear to be more insoluble. Could it be, then, that an explanation for life's origin lies outside the realm of mechanistic science? Could biology today be in a similar position to that of physics in the 1930s, when the mechanical explanation of the world was found to be inadequate? Maybe we must now return to a supernatural science in order to explain the ultimate origin of life.

Mechanistic science can offer four possible scenarios for the origin of life. These have been discussed in the preceding chapters but may be enumerated as follows:

(i)   chemical evolution in the primeval soup;

(ii) chemical evolution in interstellar space followed by accidental seeding of the earth;

(iii) continuous spontaneous creation of life in specific sites on the earth's surface;

(iv) life sent to the earth from a distant planet elsewhere in the universe.

Let us now briefly summarize some of the main difficulties with each of these theories. Firstly, let us begin with the last. Is it realistic to believe that life came here from a distant planet, either on a meteorite, a super-spaceship (as Crick would have it), or on the boot of an extra-terrestrial astronaut? Each of these suggestions is as probable as the others, although the last-mentioned makes better science fiction. Indeed, science fiction is what they are. As Weismann remarked, as long ago as 1881, 'Mere shifting of the origin of life to some other far off world cannot in any way help us.' This view is reiterated by V. A. Firsoff in his book *Life Beyond the Earth* (1963): 'The greatest weakness of any explanation by implantation from without is that it does not really solve the problem of the origin of life; it merely "passes the buck" for life would still have arisen elsewhere at some time and this would have to be explained.'[3]

Much the same may be said about the second theory, namely the evolution of life in space rather than on the earth. Thus the more it becomes recognized that chemical evolution is highly implausible because of the large number of improbable processes involved, the more necessary it becomes to speculate that maybe a solution is more possible if one brings in a greater diversity of sites and conditions offered by other planets, comets or meteors. Those who have adopted such a stance have had their judgement clouded and their reason taken prisoner. These comments also apply to those who believe that life arises today by spontaneous generation. Again this is scientific escapism.

This leaves us only the first alternative, the primeval soup theory. As I have previously pointed out, this was a light-headed suggestion of J. B. S. Haldane, which he never expected to be taken seriously. Yet it happened to appeal to a large number of people who, at that time, were trying to find an acceptable answer to the origin of life problem. Up to this time it had been a gaping flaw in Darwinian dogma. So, although verging on the pseudo-scientific, it was nonetheless welcomed with a ready eagerness by most scientists. The upshot was that the doctrine of the primeval soup soon became incorporated into modern thought. Its position was given a further boost in the early 1950s when Stanley Miller's experiments were contrived so as to offer it confirmation.

If we look back from our position today we can see that in fact Miller's work gave only minimal support for Haldane's suggestion. Despite this it was widely promulgated that the primeval soup theory was now proven and it soon became deeply entrenched in twentieth-century science.

I have discussed previously in Chapter 3 the reasons why I believe the primeval soup theory to be an elaborate fantasy. If I am correct, one is immediately led to ask the question: 'How could it be that such a fallacious concept has become incorporated into scientific orthodoxy?' To answer this question we must enquire into the nature of scientific progress and in particular seek to discover why certain scientific theories, although erroneous, become acceptable. I believe three factors are significant:

(i)   The influence and prestige of their principal proponents.

(ii) They are particularly opportune and happen to serve some non-scientific purpose.

(iii) Because there happens to be no other reasonable theory they become locked into orthodoxy.

Let me illustrate these ideas with some specific examples. One of the best examples of the first in recent years has been that of polywater. In the late 1960s the Russian physicist Boris Derjaguin believed he had isolated a new type of water which he discovered in fine silica capillaries. He gave it the name 'polywater' and it became an overnight sensation that strangely turned to panic. The *Manchester Evening News* for 11 July 1970 proclaimed the headline: 'New Polywater Can Destroy Earth Life.'

One of the principal reasons why the polywater bubble took off was because one of its earliest supporters was Professor J. D. Bernal. Bernal like Haldane, was a convinced Marxist. It is very likely that he had been badly shaken by the Lysenko affair which had taken place in the USSR a few years previously. This had damaged Russian scientific credibility in Western eyes. Bernal was desperate to find in any Soviet scientific breakthrough a way for their redemption and polywater gave him this possibility. He accordingly expended considerable energy in publicizing polywater and for a brief period enjoyed considerable success. It was all too good to be true and the bursting of the polywater bubble became inevitable. When the initial euphoria had subsided and scientists began calmly to examine what they had found they discovered that polywater was simply an aqueous solution of silica derived from the type of glass used in the experiment. Its fall from grace was precipitous and today polywater is remembered as the most ephemeral scientific discovery of the twentieth century. One American physical chemist remarked: 'We must conclude that all polywater is polycrap and that scientists have been wasting their time studying this subject.'[4]

In retrospect, it is clear that many scientists had believed in polywater because they wanted it to exist. However, the role played by J. D. Bernal in the whole saga was of crucial significance. He was one of the most eminent physical scientists of the day and without his influence polywater would not have seen the light of day. Bernal's motives, however, were far from science, they were blatantly political. This takes us to the second factor that influences the success of a scientific theory, namely, does it serve some other non-scientific purpose?

There can be no better example of this in the annals of science than the notorious N-ray affair that occurred in the early years of this present century. A full account of this extraordinary affair may be found in I. M. Klotz's book *Diamond Dealers and Feather Merchants* (1986). The salient points are as follows: at the close of the nineteenth century there existed intense rivalry between French and German scientists. This was intensified with the tremendous boost given to German science by the discovery of X-rays. One French physicist, Blondlot, was particularly grieved that the discovery of X-rays had eluded French scientists. So much so that he announced the discovery of so-called N-rays, named after the city of Nancy wherein the great discovery had been made. There was immediate rejoicing among French scientists who took up the study of N-rays with passionate fervour. To appreciate the vigour that ensued one need only consult the leading French scientific journal *Comptes Rendus* for the year 1904 to discover that the number of papers published on N-rays outnumbered those on X-rays by about 20:1. Scientists in other parts of the world treated N-rays with rather less credulity. Eventually the cat was let out of the bag by an American scientist, R. W. Wood, who went to visit Blondlot in his laboratory to observe at first hand the so-called N-rays. While he stood in the darkened laboratory he adroitly took a crucial aluminium prism from Blondlot's apparatus and placed it in his coat pocket. To his astonishment Blondlot's experiment proceeded as if the prism were still in place. One commentator later expressed what many others must have felt: 'What a spectacle for French Science that one of its distinguished savants determines the position of lines in the spectrum while the prism sits in the pocket of his American colleague.'[5]

The N-ray fiasco clearly demonstrates that particular scientific ideas are developed and promulgated for reasons that have nothing to do with science. With some, for example the N-rays, they are doomed to failure, whereas with others, there is no prism to slip into one's pocket and so they are extremely difficult to falsify. Accordingly they become incorporated into scientific orthodoxy.

Developments in science are not only determined by the motivation of a select number of chosen gurus, but by the particular circumstances of the day, which may themselves have little actual relevance to science. In the light of these comments, how may we account for the success of the primeval soup theory?

Right from its conception the primeval soup theory had all the ingredients for success. In the first place, one of its most passionate proselytizers was J. B. S. Haldane, a most influential, albeit notorious, scientist of the day. Haldane, apart from being a crank and perhaps even a little insane, belonged to a breed of militant atheists, as did Bernal, Oparin and Huxley. [6] He knew that if the Darwinist doctrine was to be successful then it was essential to have a naturalistic explanation for the origin of life. To his amazement he found other scientists eager to accept the primeval soup theory. On this point, David Hall, Professor of Philosophy at Wisconsin University, has remarked that one of the great puzzles in science is how certain scientists succeed in converting their fellow scientists when all their predecessors fail. I believe it happened in this instance simply because there was no other alternative and that most scientists would accept anything rather than invoke a final cause.

This brings us to the final reason why obscure and unreasonable ideas become incorporated into scientific orthodoxy, namely, because there is no alternative. The classic example of this is phlogiston.

Many of the early chemists believed that all inflammable materials contained a substance called phlogiston. Thus, when a material was burnt it released phlogiston; so, for instance, when a burning candle was observed to go out when placed in an enclosed jar, it was said that it did so because the air had become saturated with the substance phlogiston. This absurd explanation was accepted for many centuries simply because there was no other explanation. It was not until Joseph Priestley's discovery of oxygen that the foolishness of the phlogiston idea became evident. However, until then the phlogiston concept was locked into orthodoxy and made to agree with observation.

In a similar way, Haldane's primeval soup theory and Oparin's experimental work on coacervates have become locked into modern orthodoxy simply because there is no other mechanistic explanation for the origin of life. This situation has been greatly assisted to some extent by deliberate obscurantism.

Contrary to what is generally believed, Miller's experiments did not provide evidence for the primeval soup theory. The amino acids formed in his sparking experiments were all racemic, whereas all living organisms employ only one particular enantiomer. Furthermore, the great bulk of the amino acids formed in this type of work are not found in the proteins associated with life. What the Miller work did was to erect an impenetrable smoke-screen around the theory. To see the consequence, one only has to refer to an elementary textbook in the biological sciences to find prominently stated that the Miller experiment actually *proves* that life was created in this way.

One must admit in mitigation that we are, of course, dealing with a particularly difficult interdisciplinary area where many chemists have been dismissive in concluding that it is really biology and vice versa. In consequence, many individuals have gained only a superficial notion of the real significance of the Miller experiment. They have heard of the formation of amino acids and have been quick to assume that this is only one step away from proteins, which are themselves a little removed from life itself. But, oh how wrong is this type of extrapolation!

I believe the argument so far has gone a long way to undermine the primeval soup theory. But where does this leave us? If we cannot explain the origin of life mechanistically, then the entire edifice of Darwinism is brought into doubt. Darwin himself unscrupulously pointed to a Creator to set off the evolutionary process. We find in the first edition of the *Origin of Species* the following: 'Therefore, I should infer from analogy that probably all the organic beings which have ever lived on this earth have descended from some one primordial form, into which life was first breathed by the Creator.'[7]

However, after the theory became generally accepted he removed all reference to a Creator. Undoubtedly Darwin's behaviour has beguiled many individuals to believe that one may hold on to a belief in a Creator and at the same time accept his theory of evolution. But if one needs a Creator to form the first cell, one may just as easily have a Creator to create life as it is evident to us today. Anyway, the sort of Creator who makes the first organism and then absents himself while it evolves by blind chance is surely incompatible with the idea of a personal God.

I believe we must abandon the search for life's origin if it approaches the problem with an initial assumption of evolution. Biological evolution by its very nature is not capable of experimental verification, so must always remain an assumption. To deduce how life may have arisen from such an uncertain foundation is to tread water. If one were fortunate enough to have made a correct assumption, then one ought to be able, *by now*, to see some way out of the problem. Floundering and near capsize are surely indications that an error has been made in one's initial assumption.

Rather, we should look at what we know for certain and take it from there. Let us begin with a typical simple cell. What does it consist of? In fact, due to the recent advances in molecular biology, this is answered relatively easily. It is generally agreed now that there would be around 2000 different proteins, many of which would be enzymes. There would also be numerous nucleic acid molecules, both DNA, carrying the genetic information, and RNA molecules. Many of the RNA molecules would have a distinct functional role and would not be transposable with either the DNA or any of the protein molecules.

To envisage what the first cell was like we must try and answer the question: 'What are the minimum molecular constituents for a cell to be alive?' Yet this question is not as difficult to answer as one might expect. For if we look at a typical virus, which is not alive, we may deduce that the minimum for a cell to be alive must be something rather more. Now a simple virus might possess around forty different protein molecules, some of which might have an enzymic role and others a structural function. Together with these will be a large nucleic acid molecule, either a DNA or RNA. Accordingly from this standpoint we may now confidently predict that the first cell must have possessed more than this. The problem remains how could this, the barest minimum for life, have come together by chance alone?

Many people have made a fundamental mistake in believing that molecules themselves may develop by natural selection. They cannot. Molecules simply do not evolve. On the contrary, large molecules always break down and decompose. One is therefore forced to postulate that those unique giant molecules that went to make up the first cell must have come together at some instant in time to give a living organism. At this point we encounter formidable difficulties, for we are unable to explain how even just *one* of those giant molecules may have formed.

Let us suppose that the first cell contained around 200 different proteins, each consisting of 200 amino acids. This requires a total of 40,000 unique amino acid arrangements put together by pure chance! The probability of this happening is so remote that we may say with confidence that it is simply impossible. But the problem does not rest there. It is not enough to require that the amino acids line up in the correct order; one also must have the DNA line up so as to code for those 200 different proteins. This means several million nucleotides coming together to give the requisite sequence. If the first requirement was concluded to be impossible, this second requirement is incredible. But this is not the end of it: one also has to postulate the existence of a mechanism of converting the information from the DNA into that of the proteins. For all these three requirements to come together at one instant in time is just unbelievable.

Other scientists have also reached the same conclusion and have argued that life could not therefore have arisen by any naturalistic mechanism. Today some of these scientists are returning to the doctrine of special creation. This must, inevitably, imply the eventual demise of Darwinism. To employ a metaphor from Bunyan's famous allegory, mankind for the past century has been entombed by Darwin in Doubting Castle. During this time, we have witnessed an appalling period in human history. This has encompassed two devastating world wars and the Holocaust — both to some extent sparked off by Darwinian doctrine. We have indeed been shown the 'skulls and bones' of the Castle yard. Even today we see the widespread slaughter of innocents in legalized abortion. And the tragedy of AIDS brings home further the consequences of rejecting the truth of the Bible. 'What a fool we have been to lie in this stinking Dungeon!' exclaimed Christian, when he realized he had within his bosom the key to liberty.

Today we now have the key with which to escape from the despair of Darwinism. It lies in the science of molecular biology. This reveals that life could not have originated by chance in any primeval soup, or by any other naturalistic mechanism. But it goes much further. It reveals to us that all organisms have been designed. Furthermore, they have been designed according to a plan. And as William Paley argued, where there is design there must be a designer. *Special creation is therefore now a fact.*

Having now obtained this key to liberty, we should cast off the shackles of Darwinism and move on in faith and hope for a better future.

Appendix

The alphabet of life

Although there are now known to be thousands upon thousands of biochemicals, most of them are constructed from a small number of basic building blocks. One can draw the simple analogy to a child's Lego set, in which there are a small number of different types of block, but the number of models that could be constructed with them is infinite. So it is with the biochemistry of life. Thus to understand it one doesn't need to delve into its complex depths. All that is necessary is an elementary appreciation of the type and nature of the basic units. I have called the basic building blocks of biochemistry the 'alphabet of life'. In all there are less than three dozen different substances that when arranged in different ways go to give us 'life' as we see it around us in the world. Thus the winter snowdrop, the blackbird in the morning and the new-born baby are all constructed from the same building blocks. These building units may be divided into four groups of biochemicals, in which the members of each group have many features in common. They are: (1) amino acids; (2) sugars; (3) lipids; (4) nucleotides.

1. Amino acids

The most essential structural component of life is protein. Proteins are all constructed from some twenty different building blocks, or units, which are called *amino acids*. Amino acids have the general formula:

$$\underset{\substack{|\\ \text{COOH}}}{\overset{\substack{\text{NH}_2\\|}}{\text{R}-\text{C}-\text{H}}} \rightleftharpoons \underset{\substack{|\\ \text{COO}^-}}{\overset{\substack{\text{NH}_3^+\\|}}{\text{R}-\text{C}-\text{H}}}$$

They therefore resemble each other with the exception of the side chain R. Variation in R may give rise to an infinite variety of amino acids; however, in all living creatures only twenty variants are employed in the construction of protein. These are illustrated in Figure 13. With the exception of the simplest, glycine (R = H), each amino acid has at least one asymmetric carbon atom and so is optically active. All of the amino acids found in proteins are of the L-type. As amino acids contain both an amino group ($-NH_2$) and an acid group ($-COOH$), when placed in water these groups become ionized and the resulting form is known as *zwitterion*. It is this unique feature of amino acids that renders them soluble in water and which is so vitally important for life to occur.

2. Sugars

The sugars, or carbohydrates, are among the most abundant components of all animal and plant tissue. The name 'carbohydrate' is derived from the fact that sugars have the general formula $C_n H_{2n} O_n$ that is, sucrose is $C_{12} H_{22} O_{11}$ and glucose $C_6 H_{12} O_6$. The early chemists looked at this formula as $C_n (H_2O)$ and so called a sugar 'hydrate of carbon', hence 'carbohydrate'. Table sugar is known as 'sucrose', and as everyone is aware, it is a colourless crystalline solid with a sweet taste. All other sugars have similar properties.

In animal cells sugars are required as an essential source of energy, whereas in plants they play a structural role.

Carbohydrates may be divided into three main groups:

1. Monosaccharides (simple sugars), for example, glucose. Monosaccharides cannot be broken down into simpler sugars.

2. Disaccharides, e.g. sucrose, may be broken down with dilute acid into two simpler monosaccharides. Sucrose (table sugar) on treatment with a dilute acid breaks down into glucose and fructose.

FIGURE 13

The twenty amino acids found in all proteins

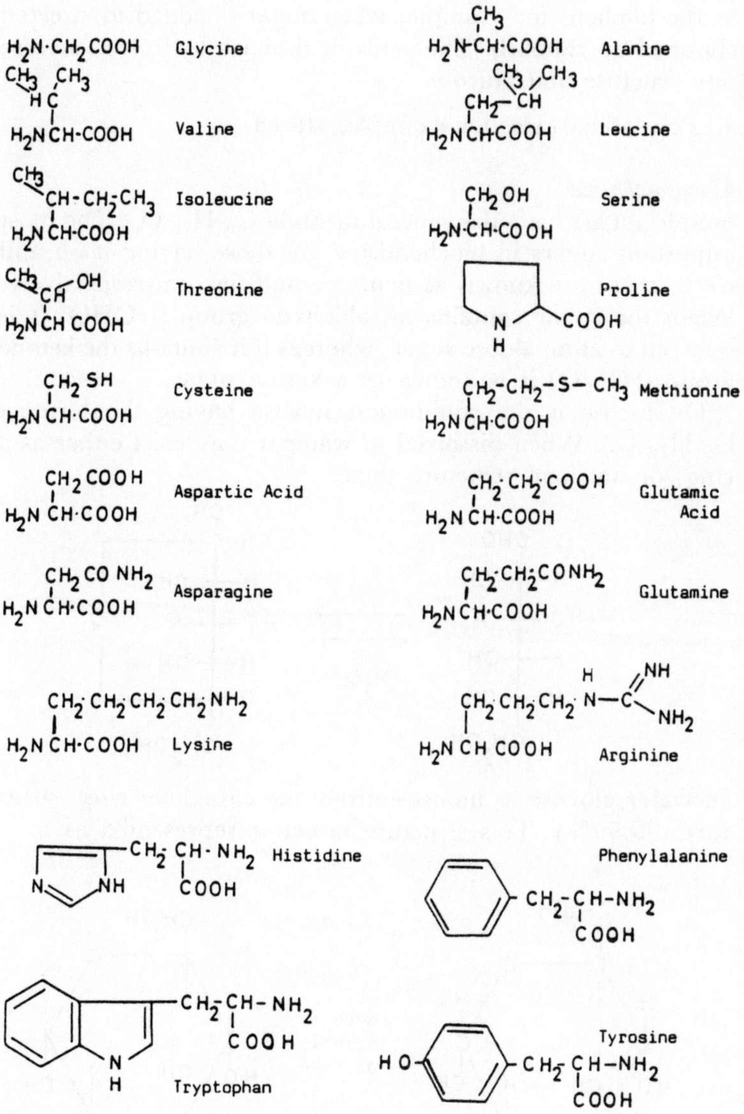

$H_2N \cdot CH_2 COOH$ Glycine

$H_2N-CH-COOH$ with CH_3 Alanine

$H_2N CH-COOH$ with CH_3 CH_3 / HC Valine

$H_2N CHCOOH$ with CH_3 CH_3 / CH_2-CH Leucine

$H_2N CH-COOH$ with CH_3 / $CH-CH_2 CH_3$ Isoleucine

$H_2N-CH-COOH$ with $CH_2 OH$ Serine

$H_2N CH COOH$ with $CH_3 CH OH$ Threonine

Proline $\begin{array}{c} N \\ H \end{array}$ COOH

$H_2N CH \cdot COOH$ with $CH_2 SH$ Cysteine

$H_2N CH \cdot COOH$ with $CH_2-CH_2-S-CH_3$ Methionine

$H_2N CH \cdot COOH$ with $CH_2 COOH$ Aspartic Acid

$H_2N CH \cdot COOH$ with $CH_2 CH_2 COOH$ Glutamic Acid

$H_2N CH \cdot COOH$ with $CH_2 CO NH_2$ Asparagine

$H_2N CH \cdot COOH$ with $CH_2 CH_2 CONH_2$ Glutamine

$H_2N CH \cdot COOH$ with $CH_2 CH_2 CH_2 CH_2 NH_2$ Lysine

$H_2N CH COOH$ with $CH_2 CH_2 CH_2 N-C \begin{array}{c} NH \\ NH_2 \end{array}$ Arginine

$\begin{array}{c} N \\ NH \end{array}$—$CH_2 CH-NH_2$ with $COOH$ Histidine

Phenylalanine $CH_2-CH-NH_2$ with $COOH$

$CH_2 CH-NH_2$ with $COOH$ Tryptophan

Tyrosine $H O$—$CH_2 CH-NH_2$ with $COOH$

sucrose   ➤   glucose   +   fructose
(disaccharide) Acid (monosaccharide)   (monosaccharide)

This is a chemical reaction frequently performed unwittingly in the kitchen, for example, when sugar is added to sweeten chopped-up rhubarb. The acids in rhubarb hydrolyse sucrose into fructose and glucose.

3. Polysaccharides, for example, starch.

Monosaccharides
Simple sugars have the general formula $C_n H_{2n} O_n$. The most important sugars in biochemistry are those having $n = 5$ and $n = 6$; these are known as pentoses and hexoses respectively. When the sugar contains an aldehyde group (–CHO) it is referred to as an aldose sugar, whereas if it contains the ketone group ($\rangle C = O$) it is known as a ketose sugar.

D-Glucose is the commonest hexose having the formula $C_6 H_{12} O_6$. When dissolved in water it may exist either as a ring, or an open structure thus:

In water glucose is almost entirely the closed, or ring, structure (99.99%). This structure is better represented as:

Ketose sugars e.g. fructose, may be similarly represented as a ring structure thus:

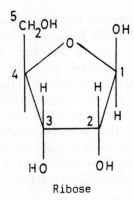

Pentose sugars have the general formula $C_5 H_{10} O_5$. Ribose is the most important and occurs in the nucleic acid RNA. In DNA a modified ribose occurs which has the oxygen removed from the 2-deoxyribose ('deoxy' meaning without oxygen, and '2-deoxy' meaning without oxygen at position number 2).

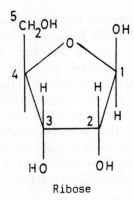

Ribose

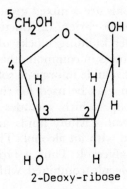

2-Deoxy-ribose

Disaccharides

Monosaccharides may combine together to form chains of sugars known as polysaccharides. When only two sugars are joined together it is known as a disaccharide. Sucrose is a typical disaccharide formed from one molecule of glucose and one of fructose, and has the structure:

Of all organic substances, sucrose has the greatest world production. It is obtained from either sugar cane or sugar beet. On a smaller scale the honeybee obtains sucrose from the nectar of flowers and converts it into honey, which is a mixture of glucose and fructose.

Other common disaccharides are maltose, which occurs in germinating cereals and malt; lactose, which is found in milk, and is produced on a commercial scale as a by-product of cheese manufacture; and cellobiose, which is obtained during the hydrolysis of wood.

3. Lipids

Lipids are a mixed group of substances that are important for a wide variety of functions within the living cell. Unlike the other building blocks of life, as a group they have very few features in common other than being largely insoluble in water, but soluble in organic solvents such as chloroform. This distinction may be used for the basis of a working definition of the group, which includes waxes, fats, vegetable oils and the steroids. Many lipids are esters, that is a combination of an acid with an alcohol. The most abundant lipids are the esters of glycerol. Thus a typical animal fat consists of a glycerol molecule combined with three molecules of a fatty acid.

$$CH_2OH \qquad\qquad CH_2OA'$$
$$|\qquad\qquad\qquad\quad |$$
$$CH\ OH \qquad\qquad CH\ O\ A''$$
$$|\qquad\qquad\qquad\quad |$$
$$CH_2OH \qquad\qquad CH_2O\ A'''$$

Glycerol   a fat
                (where A is a fatty acid)

The fatty acids A', A", and A''' may all be identical, or different. If they are all stearic acid, for example, the fat is known as tristearin, a common lipid of animal tissue.

Fatty acids resemble acetic acid (CH_3COOH), only the side chain is a long hydrocarbon chain; stearic acid, for instance, has the formula: $CH_3 (CH_2)_{16} COOH$. Fatty acids have the general formula $CH_3 (CH_2)_n COOH$. Such an acid is said to be 'saturated' and a fat containing such acids would be described as a 'saturated fat'. On the other hand, unsaturated fatty acids exist and may contain one or more double bonds, for example, oleic acid has the formula: $CH_3 (CH_2)_7 CH = CH (CH_2)_7 COOH$.

Animal fats contain mainly saturated fatty acids. Butter, for instance, is composed of a mixture of saturated animal fats. Vegetable oils, on the other hand, consist predominantly of unsaturated fatty acids, olive oil, for example. These oils may be treated with hydrogen gas to convert the unsaturated fatty acid components into the saturated form. In this transformation the oil is converted into a solid, of which margarine is an example.

Lipids because they are insoluble in water make up the principal components of animal cell membranes. They form an envelope within which all the vital processes of living occur and at the same time they exclude entry to foreign and unwanted substances.

Steroids are also members of the lipid family, mainly by virtue of their similar water solubility properties. They have extremely complex structures and occur in living organisms as hormones, as well as important constituents of cell membranes. They therefore have an important role to play in metabolism. The steroid structure is based on a pattern of seventeen carbon atoms linked together to give four interlocking rings. The main steroid of animal cells is cholesterol. As most people are now aware, derivatives of this lipid are believed to deposit in the veins and arteries of man ultimately contributing to the development of coronary heart disease. We are now all familiar with so-called low-cholesterol level diets.

Other steroids, which all have a similar structure to cholesterol, include vitamin D, the bile salts and many hormones including the sex hormones.

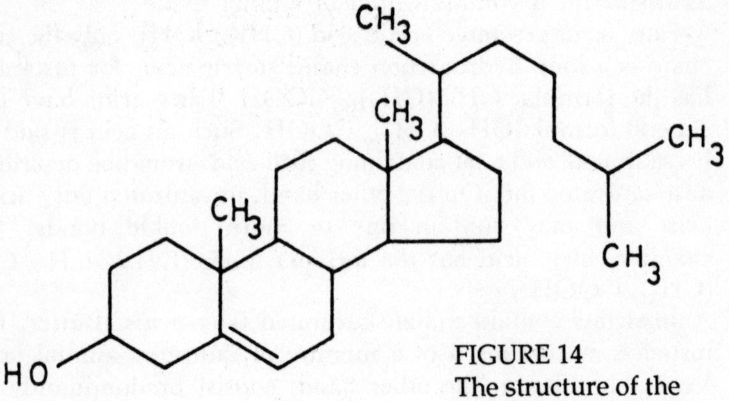

FIGURE 14
The structure of the
cholesterol molecule.
Four rings are fused
together with various
side chains.

4. Nucleotides

Nucleic acids are giant molecules responsible for the transmission of heredity. They are built up of linear chains of subunits known as *nucleotides*. Thus a nucleic acid may be thought of as a polymer of a nucleotide (N), thus . . . N-N-N-N-N-N-N . . . etc. The nucleotide N is itself built up of three substances: (1) an organic base, (2) a sugar, and (3) a molecule of phosphoric acid. A nucleotide is therefore equal to: Base + Sugar + H_3PO_4.

There are five organic bases employed in the construction of nucleic acids. They are either derivatives of pyrimidine (one ring) or purine (two rings).

They are: cytosine, uracil, thymine (all derivatives of pyrimidine); and adenine, guanine (both derivatives of purine).

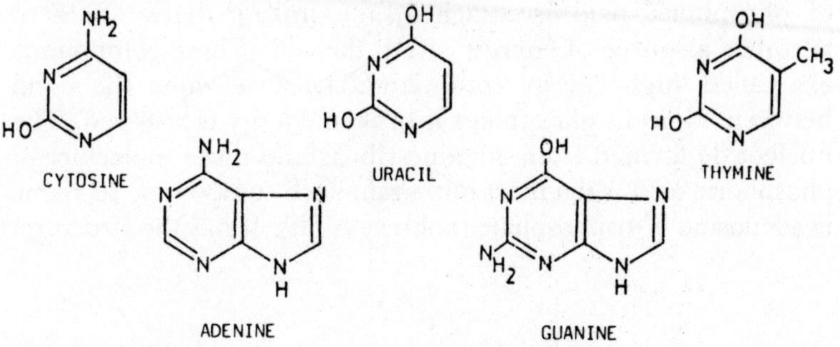

CYTOSINE   URACIL   THYMINE

ADENINE   GUANINE

The nucleotides present in RNA contain the sugar D-ribose, whereas those from DNA contain D-2-deoxyribose.

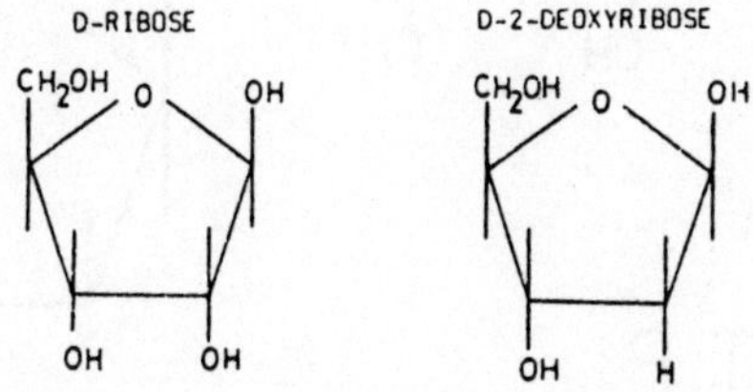

D-RIBOSE   D-2-DEOXYRIBOSE

In addition, the nucleotides from either RNA or DNA contain phosphoric acid (H_3PO_4) attached either to the 5' or 3' hydroxyl group of the sugar.

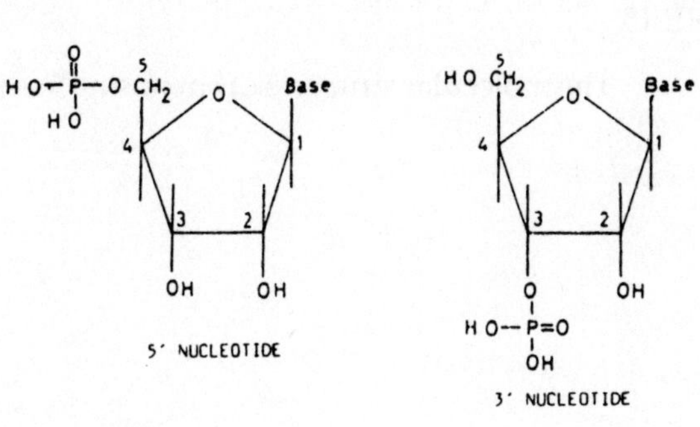

5' NUCLEOTIDE   3' NUCLEOTIDE

Apart from their presence in nucleic acids nucleotides play an essential role in cell metabolism. When more than one unit of phosphoric acid is attached, the linkage between them becomes a source of energy within the cell. These compounds are called 'high energy compounds' because when the bond between adjacent phosphates is broken energy is released. The nucleotide formed from adenine-ribose and three molecules of phosphoric acid is the most important such compound. Its name is adenosine-5′-triphosphate (abbrev. ATP). It has the structure:

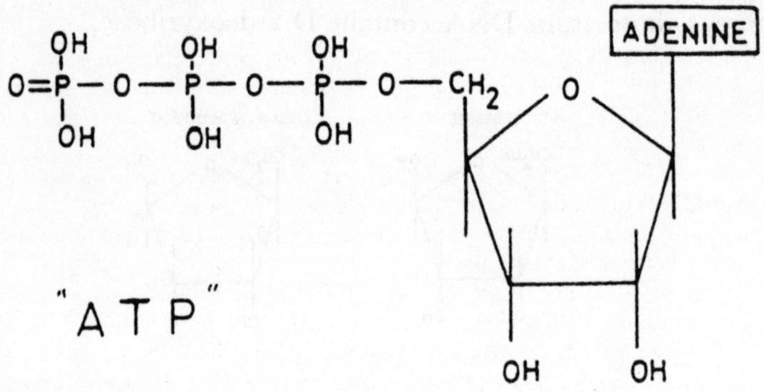

FIGURE 15

The molecular structure of adenosine 5'-triphosphate

Bibliography

Arrhenius S. (1908), *Worlds in the Making*, Harper & Row, London.

Barrow, J.D. and Tipler, F.J. (1986), *The Anthropic Cosmological Principle*, Clarendon Press, Oxford.

Bastian, H.C. (1911), *The Origins of Life*, Watts & Co., London.

Bernal, J.D. (1967), *The Origins of Life*, Weidenfeld & Nicholson, London.

Breuer, R. (1982), *Contact with the Stars: the Search for Extraterrestrial Life*, W.H. Freeman.

Cairns-Smith, A.G. (1982), *Genetic Takeover and the Mineral Origins of Life*, Cambridge University Press, Cambridge.

Cairns-Smith, A.G. (1985), *Seven Clues to the Origin of Life*, Cambridge University Press, Cambridge.

Cairns-Smith, A.G. and Hartman, H. (1987), *Clay Minerals and the Origin of Life*, Cambridge University Press, Cambridge.

Clark, R. (1968), *'J.B.S.'*, Hodder and Stoughton, London.

Claus, G. and Madri, P.P. (1972), *Annals of New York Academy Science.*

Crick, F. (1982), *Life Itself — Its Origin and Nature*, Futura, London.

Darwin, C. (1903), *On the Origin of Species by means of Natural Selection*, (Reprint of the first edition) Watts & Co., London.

Darwin, E. (1803), *The Temple of Nature*, J. Johnson, London.

Darwin, F. and Seward, A.C. (Eds) (1903), *More Letters of C. Darwin,* J. Murray, London.

Dawkins, R. (1986), *The Blind Watchmaker, Longman, London.*

Dyson, F. (1985), *Origins of Life*, Cambridge University Press, Cambridge.

Farley, J. (1974), *The Spontaneous Generation Controversy*, John Hopkins University Press.

Firsoff, V.A. (1963), *Life Beyond the Earth — A Study in Exobiology,* Hutchinson, London.

Fox, S.W. (1965) (Ed.), *The Origins of Prebiological Systems*, Academic Press, London.

Haldane, J.B.S. (1929), *Rationalist Annual.*

Hoyle, F. (1983), *The Intelligent Universe*, M. Joseph, London.

Hoyle, F. and Wickramasinghe, C. (1978), *Lifecloud*, Dent & Son, London.

Hoyle, F. and Wickramasinghe, C. (1979), *Diseases from Space*, Dent & Son, London.

Hoyle, F. and Wickramasinghe, C. (1981), *Space Travellers*, University College Cardiff Press, Cardiff.

Hoyle, F. and Wickramasinghe, C. (1984), *From Grains to Bacteria*, University College Cardiff Press, Cardiff.

Irvine, W. (1956), *Apes Angels and Victorians*, Weidenfeld and Nicolson, London.

Jaki, S.L. (1981), *Cosmos and Creator*, Scottish Academic Press, Edinburgh.

Klotz, I.M. (1986), *Diamond Dealers and Feather Merchants*, Birkhauser.

Margulis, L. (1970), *Origin of Eukaryotic Cells*, Yale University Press.

Margulis, L. (1981), *Symbiosis in Cell Evolution*, W.H. Freeman.

Miller, S.L. (1953), *Science 117*, p.528.

Miller, S.L. (1986), *Chemica Scripta, 26B* pp.5–11.

Orgel, L.E. (1973), *The Origins of Life*, John Wiley, New York.

Paley, W. (1826), *Natural Theology, or Evidences of the Existence and Attributes of the Deity*, J. Vincent, Oxford.

Pirie, N.W. (1986), *Comprehensive Biochemistry*, vol. 36 pp.517.

Scott, A. (1987), *The Creation of Life*, Blackwell, Oxford.

Shapiro, R. (1986), *Origins — A Skeptic's Guide to the Creation of Life on Earth*, Heinemann, London.

Wald, G. (1964), The Origins of Life, *Proc. Natl. Acad. Sci. USA, 52*, pp.595–611.

Notes

Preface

1. E. J. Wood and W. R. Pickering, *Introducing Biochemistry*, (1982), p.17 (John Murray, London).

Introduction

1. F. Dyson (1985), p.31.
2. F. Hoyle and N. C. Wickramasinghe (1981), p.32.
3. *Dictionary of National Biography* (1961–70), p.474.
4. W. Paley (1826), p.8.

Chapter 1

1. J. Priestley (1809), *Trans Am.phil.Soc.*, *6*, 119.
2. J. B. S. Haldane, in Fox (1965), p.12.
3. C. Darwin (1903).
4. cf. F. Darwin and A. C. Seward (1903), vol. 1, p.172.
5. H. C. Bastian (1911), p.5.
6. cf. *Nature* (1987), *329* p.104, and (1986) *322*, p.206.
7. C. Ponnamperuma in *New Scientist*, May 1982.
8. T. Hardy, in *Tess of the d'Urbervilles*, ch.19.

Chapter 3

1. S. L. Miller, *Science* (1953) *117*, p.528.
2. cf. D. E. Hull, *Nature* (1960), *186*, pp.693–4.
3. A. G. Cairns-Smith (1982).
4. A. G. Cairns-Smith (1982), p.56.
5. cf. R. M. Lemmon, 'Chemical Evolution' in *Chem. Rev.*, (1970) *70*, p.95.
6. A. G. Cairns-Smith (1982), p.62.
7. Old English term for fools, from the legend of 'the wise men' of Gotham, a small village near Nottingham.
8. cf. G. Wald (1964).
9. A. G. Cairns-Smith (1982), p.63.
10. cf. W. Irvine (1956), p.253.

Chapter 4

1. cf. *Nature* (1977) *268*, pp.71–73.
2. B. Norden, 'The Asymmetry of Life', *J. Mol. Evolution* (1978) *11*, p.313.
3. cf. D. W. Gidley *et al., Nature* (1982) *297*, p.639, and R. A. Hegstrom *et al., Nature* (1985) *313*, p.391.

Chapter 5

1. F. Crick (1982), p.143.

Chapter 6

1. Report in *Chemistry in Britain*, January 1983, p.18.
2. N. W. Pirie, review of *Molecular Evolution & Origin of Life* (1972) by S. Fox and K. Dose.
3. Stephen Moreton, *Daily Telegraph*, 6 December 1986.
4. A. G. Cairns-Smith (1982), p.130.
5. *ibid.*, p.130.
6. R. Dawkins (1986).

Chapter 7

1. F. Crick (1982), p.81.
2. F. Dyson (1985), p.24.
3. *ibid.*, p.9.
4. cf. *Nature*, (1983) *301*, pp.618–620.

Chapter 8

1. F. Crick (1982), p.88.
2. *ibid.*, p.150.

Chapter 9

1. J. J. Berzelius, *Ann.Phys.Chem.*, (1834) *33*, p.113.
2. G. Claus and P. P. Madri, p.391.
3. *ibid.*, p.390.
4. *ibid.*, p.394.
5. *ibid.*, p.395.
6. N. W. Pirie, *Phil. Trans. Roy. Soc.*, (1981), A303, p.592.
7. *Nature*, (1970), *228*, p.923.
8. cf. CETI by J. Stanley, Wyndham Pub. (1976).
9. cf. *Nature*, (1982) *296*, p.837.

Chapter 10

1. cf. *Nature*, (1981), *294*, p.105.
2. F. Hoyle and N. C. Wickramasinghe (1979), p.4.
3. F. Hoyle and N. C. Wickramasinghe (1978), p.26.
4. F. Hoyle and N. C. Wickramasinghe (1981), p.83.
5. Report by P. Newmark, *Nature*, (1980), p.287.
6. L. B. Halstead in *Nature*, (1981), *294*, p.484.
7. F. Hoyle and N. C. Wickramasinghe (1981), p.32.

Chapter 11

1. W. Thomson (1872), *Rep. Brit. Assoc. Adv. Sci.*, 41, lxxxiv.
2. J. D. Bernal, in Fox (Ed.) (1965), p.85.
3. cf. F. Crick, (1982), p.13.
4. J. S. Trefil, *Nature*, (1982), *300*.
5. *ibid.*
6. H. Harrison, *New Scientist*, 29 April 1982.

Chapter 12

1. F. Crick (1982), p.71.
2. A. R. Battersby (1986), *Ann N.Y. Acad. Sci.*, 463, pp.138-153.
3. E. J. Simon, *ibid.*, p.31.
4. cf. *Nature* (1986) *321*, pp.565–6.

Chapter 13

1. F. Crick (1982), p.88.
2. F. Dyson (1985), p.17.
3. V. A. Firsoff (1963), *Life Beyond the Earth*.
4. J. A. LeBel, quoted in *Nature* (1986), *322,* p.781.
5. *ibid.*
6. cf. R. Clark (1968).
7. C. Darwin (1903), p.193.

Index